Vicksburg:
Fall of the
Confederate Gibraltar

CIVIL WAR CAMPAIGNS AND COMMANDERS SERIES

Under the General Editorship of Grady McWhiney

PUBLISHED

Vicksburg:
Fall of the
Confederate Gibraltar

Terrence J. Winschel

McWhiney Foundation Press
McMurry University
Abilene, Texas

Cataloging-in-Publication Data

Winschel, Terrence J.
      Vicksburg: fall of the Confederate Gibraltar /
      Terrence J. Winschel
      p. cm. — (Civil War campaigns and commanders series)
      Includes bibliographical references and index.
      ISBN 1-893114-00-7

    1. Vicksburg (Miss.)–History–Siege, 1863. 2. United
States–History–Civil War, 1861-1865–Campaigns.
3. Mississippi–History–Civil War, 1861-1865. I. Title. II. Series

        E475.27 .W5 1999
        973.7'34   98-25133
                                                    CIP

ISBN 1-893114-00-7
10 9 8 7 6 5 4 3 2 1

Book Designed by Rosenbohm Graphic Design

All inquiries regarding volume purchases of this book should be
addressed to McWhiney Foundation Press, McMurry Station, Box 637,
Abilene, TX 79697-0637.
Telephone inquiries may be made by calling (915) 793-4682

A Note on the Series

Few segments of America's past excite more interest than Civil War battles and leaders. This ongoing series of brief, lively, and authoritative books–*Civil War Campaigns and Commanders*–salutes this passion with inexpensive and accurate accounts that are readable in a sitting. Each volume, separate and complete in itself, nevertheless conveys the agony, glory, death, and wreckage that defined America's greatest tragedy.

In this series, designed for Civil War enthusiasts as well as the newly recruited, emphasis is on telling good stories. Photographs and biographical sketches enhance the narrative of each book, and maps depict events as they happened. Sound history is meshed with the dramatic in a format that is just lengthy enough to inform and yet satisfy.

Grady McWhiney
General Editor

Dedicated in loving memory to:

Betty Mullen Winschel (1925-1996),
my beloved mother, the foundation on whom my life is built;
and
Albert Bernard Winschel (1917-1992),
my father, my friend, my inspiration.

I am so very proud to be your son.

CONTENTS

CAMPAIGNS AND COMMANDERS SERIES

Map Key

Geography

 Trees

 Marsh

 Fields

 Strategic Elevations

 Rivers

 Tactical Elevations

 Fords

 Orchards

 Political Boundaries

Human Construction

 Bridges

 Railroads

Tactical Towns

Strategic Towns

Buildings

Church

Roads

Military

 Union Infantry

 Confederate Infantry

 Cavalry

 Artillery

Headquarters

Encampments

Fortifications

Permanant Works

Hasty Works

Obstructions

Engagements

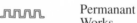 Warships

 Gunboats

 Casemate Ironclad

 Monitor

 Tactical Movements

 Strategic Movements

Maps by
Donald S. Frazier, Ph.D.
Abilene, Texas

MAPS

PHOTOGRAPHS AND ILLUSTRATIONS

Vicksburg:
Fall of the
Confederate Gibraltar

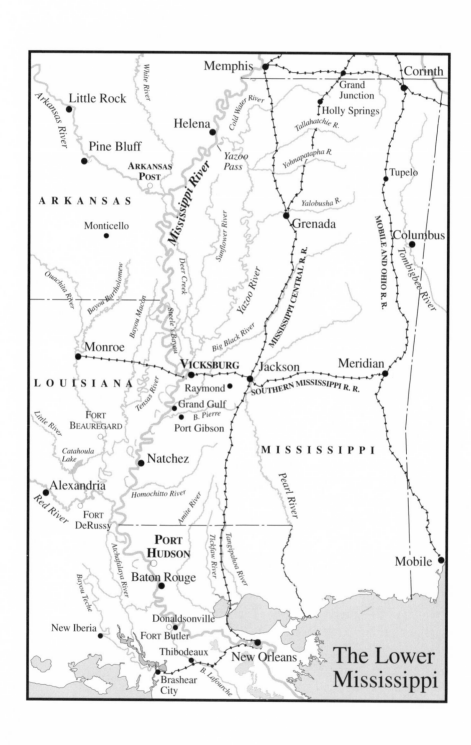

The Lower Mississippi

1

VICKSBURG IS THE KEY

Biographer and newspaperman Lloyd Lewis accurately portrayed the Mississippi River in the mid-nineteenth century as "The spinal column of America...the symbol of geographic unity." He referred to the great river as "the trunk of the American tree, with limbs and branches reaching to the Alleghenies, the Canadian border, the Rocky Mountains." For more than two thousand miles the river flows silently on its course to the sea, providing a natural artery of commerce. Gliding along the Mississippi's muddy water were steamers and flatboats of all descriptions heavily laden with rich agricultural produce en route to world markets. Indeed, the silent water of the mighty river was the single most important economic feature of the continent, the very lifeblood of America. One contemporary wrote emphatically that "The Valley of the Mississippi is America."

Upon the secession of the Southern states, and in particular Louisiana and Mississippi, the river was closed to unfettered navigation, threatening to strangle Northern commercial interests. With the advent of civil war, President Abraham Lincoln gathered his ranking civil and military leaders to discuss strategy for opening the Mississippi River and ending what he termed a "rebellion" in the Southern states. Seated at a large table Lincoln examined a map of the nation; he made a wide sweeping gesture with his hand then placed his finger on the map and said, "See what a lot of land these fellows hold, of which Vicksburg is the key. The war can never be brought to a close until that key is in our pocket." It was the president's contention that "We can take all the northern ports of the Confederacy, and they can defy us from Vicksburg. It means hog and hominy without limit, fresh troops from all the states of the far South, and a cotton country where they can raise the staple without interference." Lincoln assured his listeners that "I am acquainted with that region and know what I am talking about, and, as valuable as New Orleans will be to us, Vicksburg will be more so."

The president's powerful statements were no exaggeration. Confederate cannon mounted along the bluffs that commanded the Mississippi River at Vicksburg were not only trained on the river, but denied that important avenue of commerce to Northern shipping. Vicksburg was also the link between the eastern and western parts of the Confederacy, what Confederate President Jefferson Davis referred to as "the nailhead that held the South's two halves together." In addition, by 1862 the city sat astride a major supply route, over which the armies of Braxton Bragg and Robert E. Lee received much needed food, clothing, medicine, and other vital supplies, as well as fresh troops.

It was imperative for the Lincoln Administration to regain control of the lower Mississippi River, to enable the rich agricultural produce of the Midwest to reach world markets. Control of the river would also split the Confederacy in two,

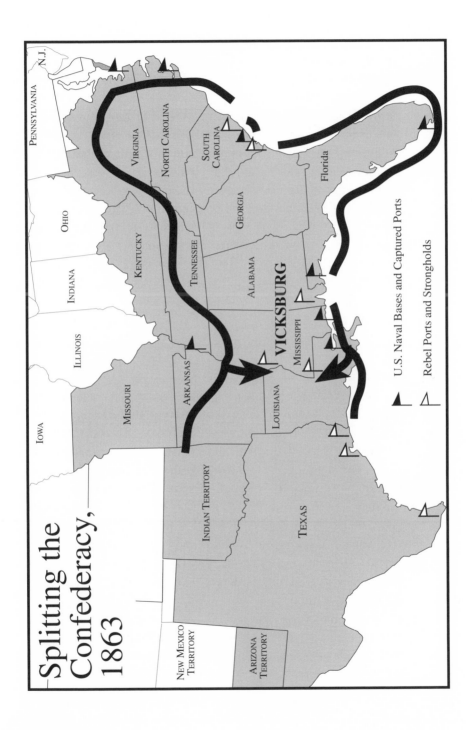

Splitting the
Confederacy,
1863

U.S. Naval Bases and Captured Ports

Rebel Ports and Strongholds

VICKSBURG

PENNSYLVANIA
N.J.
OHIO
INDIANA
ILLINOIS
IOWA
MISSOURI
KENTUCKY
VIRGINIA
NORTH CAROLINA
SOUTH CAROLINA
TENNESSEE
GEORGIA
ALABAMA
FLORIDA
MISSISSIPPI
ARKANSAS
LOUISIANA
TEXAS
INDIAN TERRITORY
NEW MEXICO TERRITORY
ARIZONA TERRITORY

sever the vital supply route, and achieve a major objective of General-in-Chief Winfield Scott's Anaconda Plan—the strategic plan by which the North would confront the Confederacy.*

WILLIAM T. SHERMAN

Born Ohio 1820; graduated from U.S. Military Academy 1840, sixth in his class; 2d lieutenant 3rd Artillery 1840; 1st lieutenant 1841; stationed in California during Mexican War; captain 1850. Resigned from army 1853 to become banker; after business failed, Sherman voluntarily assumed personal financial responsibility for money lost by his friends; practiced law for a short time in Kansas, losing only case he tried; from 1859 to 1861 superintendent of military college that later became Louisiana State University. Colonel 13th Infantry and then brigadier general volunteers 1861; commanded brigade at First Bull Run; commanded division at Shiloh; major general volunteers 1862 to 1864, serving under Grant in the Vicksburg and Chattanooga campaigns; brigadier general U.S. Army 1863; major general 1864; assumed direction of principal military operations in the West. Directed Meridian and Atlanta campaigns, March to the Sea, and Carolina campaign that ended in surrender of Joseph E. Johnston's army in 1865; received thanks of Congress "for gallant and arduous services" during the Civil War; lieutenant general 1866; general 1869; commander of the army 1869 to 1883; retired 1883; published memoirs 1875; died 1891. Made his famous statement, "war is all hell," in a speech at Columbus, Ohio, in 1880. An officer noted that Sherman's "features express determination, particularly the mouth. He is a very homely man, with a regular nest of wrinkles in his face, which play and twist as he eagerly talks on each subject; but his expression is pleasant and kindly." Some authorities rate him an even better general than Grant.

This would effectively seal the doom of Richmond.

Federal Major General William T. Sherman, a man destined to play a prominent role in the military operations against Vicksburg, wrote that "The Mississippi, source and mouth, must be controlled by one government." So firm was his belief that Sherman stated, "To secure the safety of the navigation of the Mississippi River I would slay millions. On that point I am not only insane, but mad." Major General Henry W. Halleck wrote in similarly direct, albeit less eloquent terms, "In my opinion, the opening of the Mississippi River will be to us of more advantage than the capture of forty Richmonds." Jefferson Davis, writing to Lieutenant General John C. Pemberton after the fall of Vicksburg, stated, "I thought and still think you did right to risk an army for the purpose of keeping command of even a section of the Mississippi River. Had you succeeded, none would have blamed, had you not made the attempt few would have defended your course."

In order to protect the Mississippi Valley, Confederate authorities established a line of defense that ran from Columbus, Kentucky, on the left, overlooking the Mississippi River, to Fort Henry on the Tennessee River and Fort Donelson on the Cumberland River, through Bowling Green, and on to Cumberland Gap, where the right flank was anchored on the mountains. On the great river south of Columbus, fortifications were placed at Island No. 10, and Fort Pillow was constructed on the Chickasaw Bluffs north of Memphis. Seventy miles below New Orleans, two powerful masonry forts, Forts Jackson and St. Philip, stood guard near the mouths of the Mississippi River.

---

* Scott's Anaconda Plan called for a naval blockade of Southern ports to prevent the flow of war supplies from Europe to the Confederacy, while Federal troops occupied the line of the Mississippi River, splitting the Confederacy. Thus, in the coils of the giant "Anaconda," the South could not long survive.

Eager to confront the difficult task before them, Union land and naval forces moved with a vengeance from two directions in a massive converging attack designed to wrestle the river from Confederate control. Driving south from Cairo, Illinois, Federal forces seized Forts Henry and Donelson and opened the pathway of invasion to the Deep South. Continuing the drive, Union forces gained victories at Shiloh in April 1862, at Corinth in May, and, having forced the surrender of Island No. 10 and the evacuation of Fort Pillow, they seized Memphis on June 6.

DAVID GLASGOW FARRAGUT

Born Tennessee 1801; after moving with his family to New Orleans, Farragut came under the guardianship of Captain David Porter; in 1810, at not yet ten years of age, he was appointed midshipman in the U.S. Navy; the following year he joined Porter's crew aboard the frigate *Essex*; serving in the Pacific during the War of 1812, he was appointed prize master of a captured British vessel; Farragut was actively engaged during Porter's defeat by two British warships at Valparaiso; taken prisoner, he was exchanged in November 1814; his next five years were spent on duty mostly in the Mediterranean; he studied in Tunis and, in 1825, became a lieutenant; thereafter he saw a variety of duties in the Gulf of Mexico and the south Atlantic; in 1841 he was promoted to commander and, the following year, took command of the sloop *Decatur*; he was largely left out of the action during the Mexican War; given command of the sloop *Saratoga*, he arrived too late to participate in the capture of Vera Cruz; following another period of varied assignments, during which he received promotion to captain, he was, at the outbreak of the Civil War, awaiting orders at his home in Norfolk, Virginia; with

Moving upriver from the Gulf of Mexico, the ships of the West Gulf Blockading Squadron commanded by Flag-Officer David Glasgow Farragut bombarded and passed Forts Jackson and St. Philip on April 24, capturing New Orleans thirty-six hours later. With initial success behind him, Farragut sent an advance flotilla up river. Baton Rouge fell to the Federals on May 8, Natchez four days later, and the flotilla steamed on toward Vicksburg.

After the fall of New Orleans, as the Union pincer slowly

Virginia's secession, he moved his family to New York; as a Southerner, he was initially viewed with suspicion—his only assignment in 1861 being on a retirement board; in January 1862 he was given command of the West Gulf Blockading Squadron, with the mission of capturing New Orleans; in April 1862 he did just that; with the bulk of his fleet he ran past Forts Jackson and St. Philip and captured the defenseless city in what may have been the most decisive single action of the war—one from which the Confederate government could not rebound; for this he was promoted to rear admiral; thereafter he moved up the Mississippi and, in July 1862, fought his way past Vicksburg before returning to the Gulf of Mexico; he again ascended the Mississippi to attack Port Hudson in March 1863; in July of that year he returned to New York and received a hero's welcome; he returned to the Gulf in January 1864 to begin operations against Mobile; in August 1864 his fleet engaged the Confederate Forts Morgan and Gaines; aboard his flagship *Hartford*, Farragut is reported to have exclaimed "Damn the torpedoes, full speed ahead" as he led the fleet past the forts and through a mine field—both forts capitulated by month's end; in December, suffering from poor health, he again returned to New York, where the citizens presented him with $50,000 with which to purchase a house there; he also received promotion to vice admiral; he returned to duty in the waning moments of the conflict and was among the first Federal officers to enter Richmond after its fall; in July 1866 he became the first full admiral in the nation's history; after the war he commanded the European Squadron; Admiral Farragut died at Portsmouth, New Hampshire, in 1870, still on active duty in his sixtieth year of service to the U.S. Navy.

closed along the river, the Confederates began to fortify Vicksburg. The city's geographical location made it ideal for defense. Equally important, existing rail lines that connected Vicksburg with Jackson and, via Jackson, points elsewhere in the Confederacy, enabled the shipment of heavy ordnance to the "Hill City." It was not long before Vicksburg became known as the "Gibraltar of the Confederacy," and it would prove a tough nut to crack. The strategic significance of Vicksburg greatly increased after the fall of Memphis, as it then became the northern most point below Memphis where the bluffs met the river. It was only a matter of time before war in all its horror centered on Vicksburg.

Initial efforts by Union land and naval forces to capture Vicksburg and open the great waterway to navigation ended in failure. The first threat developed on May 18, 1862, when the ships of the West Gulf Blockading Squadron arrived below Vicksburg and Federal officers demanded the city's surrender. In terse words the demand was refused. Post commander Lieutenant Colonel James L. Autry replied that "Mississippians don't know, and refuse to learn, how to surrender to an enemy." Incensed, the Federals opened fire upon the city and maintained an intermittent bombardment from late May, through June, and into late July, all to no avail. The bombardment was ineffective, and Farragut's fleet, racked with sickness and plagued by rapidly falling waters, withdrew to New Orleans and deeper waters. One Vicksburg resident, who watched the fleet withdraw, noted with jubilation, "What will they say [in the] North now about opening the Mississippi River; huzzah for Vicksburg," but added, "[nine] groans for New Orleans."

During this period, referred to as the naval siege of Vicksburg, Farragut's squadron was accompanied by a brigade of infantry commanded by Brigadier General Thomas Williams. Not willing to attempt an amphibious landing to capture the city with his small command, Williams placed his men to work with pick and shovel, excavating a canal across the base of De Soto Point, opposite Vicksburg. Intended to open an avenue of navigation that would bypass the batteries at Vicksburg, there were some who believed that the canal might cause the river to change course and leave the city high and dry, and thus render it useless militarily without firing a shot. It proved a futile effort as those who labored on the canal quickly fell victim to sun stroke, heat exhaustion, malaria, and fever. Work ceased in early July.

Also in July, the powerful Confederate ironclad ram *Arkansas*, under the command of Lieutenant Isaac N. Brown, steamed from the navy yard at Yazoo City to engage the Federal fleets in the Mississippi River. Brown caught Farragut's vessels by surprise and managed to battle his way to safety beneath the batteries at Vicksburg. In this celebrated action, the *Arkansas* suffered heavy damage but helped convince Farragut that Vicksburg could not be taken solely on the might of his naval guns.

Union and Confederate leaders understood, then and there, that if Vicksburg were to fall it would take the combined effort of Federal land and naval forces. The batteries that overlooked the Mississippi River at Vicksburg were powerful, indeed formidable, but all the land accesses were open. The Confederates determined to construct a line of defenses to guard the city's landward approaches and to control overland access to Vicksburg. Responsibility for the design and construction of these works was assigned to Major Samuel Lockett, chief engineer of the Department of Mississippi and East Louisiana. Lockett, who graduated second in his West Point class of 1859, was a highly skilled and well trained engineer. He set about his task with vigor.

Reconnoitering through the hills and hollows around Vicksburg, Lockett quickly recognized that the city was naturally defensible. Because of a series of sharp narrow ridges, fronted by steep ravines, Vicksburg was a natural fortress that he planned to make even stronger with the construction of field fortifications. The line as constructed consisted of nine major forts—redans (triangular shaped), redoubts (rectangular shaped), and lunettes (crescent shaped)—made of earth and logs and connected by a continuous line of trenches and rifle pits. The line was more than eight miles in length and formed a huge semicircle around Vicksburg, the flanks of which rested on the river above and below the city. It would be manned by a garrison of 30,000 troops, mount 172 big guns, and pose a major challenge to Union domination of the river.

The formidable nature of Vicksburg's defenses was recognized throughout the North, and not only by military leaders. A reporter for *The New York Times* observed in reference to Union operations on the Mississippi River, "We are now attempting in fact to take a mountain." The mountain was formidable, indeed a fortress, but the challenge posed by this Gibraltar would be met by a relentless and resourceful opponent.

2
BATTLE ON THE BAYOU

At 40 years of age, Major General Ulysses S. Grant could ill afford to ignore the Vicksburg challenge. An 1843 graduate of the United States Military Academy at West Point and veteran of the Mexican War, he was no stranger to confrontation and had struggled with adversity much of his adult life. Having battled his way to national prominence as commander of Federal forces at Belmont and Fort Donelson, he barely escaped disaster at Shiloh. Rumors of his drunkenness on duty, coupled with an adversarial relationship with his superior, General Halleck, resulted in Grant's demotion and almost cost him his career. But late in 1862, after the Battles of Iuka (September 19) and Corinth (October 3-4) in northern Mississippi, Grant was given command of the newly designated Army of the Tennessee—one of two major Federal field armies in the Western Theater. The initiative now swung to Grant. His objective was the Confederate stronghold on the Mississippi River—Vicksburg.

To seize the city that Lincoln called the "key" to Union victory, Grant divided his force. One column, consisting of 40,000 troops under his personal command, marched south along the line of the Mississippi Central Railroad from Grand Junction, Tennessee, into northern Mississippi. His object was to draw Confederate forces responsible for the defense of the

ULYSSES S. GRANT

Born Ohio 1822; graduated U.S. Military Academy 1843, twenty-first in his class; brevetted 2d lieutenant in 4th Infantry 1843; 2d lieutenant 1845; 1st lieutenant 1847; regimental quartermaster 1847 to 1853; brevetted captain 1847 for gallant conduct in Mexican War; assigned in 1852 to duty in California, where he missed his wife and drank heavily. Resigned from army in 1854 to avoid court martial; failed at a number of undertakings; appointed colonel 21st Illinois Infantry and then brigadier general volunteers in 1861; major general volunteers 1862; gained national attention following victories at Fort Donelson, Shiloh, and Vicksburg; received thanks of Congress and promotion to major general U.S. Army in 1863; after victories around Chattanooga, appointed lieutenant general and commander of all U.S. forces in 1864. Accompanied Meade's Army of the Potomac on a bloody campaign of attrition through the Wilderness, Spotsylvania, Cold Harbor, siege of Petersburg, and the pursuit to Appomattox; commander of the U.S. Army 1864 to 1869; U.S. president 1869 to 1877. Visited Europe, suffered bankruptcy, and wrote his memoirs while dying of cancer; died in 1885 in New York City, where he is buried. "The art of war is simple enough," Grant once explained. "Find out where your enemy is. Get at him as soon as you can. Strike at him as hard as you can, and keep moving on." A staff officer said of Grant: "His face has three expressions: deep thought, extreme determination, and great simplicity and calmness."

Vicksburg-Jackson area into the northern portion of the state and there keep them pinned while the other column, consisting of 32,000 men under Major General William T. Sherman, made a rapid amphibious thrust down the Mississippi River to seize Vicksburg.

Grant's column started the march on November 26, 1862, and slowly pushed southward through Holly Springs and Oxford toward Grenada, where Confederate forces under Lieutenant General John C. Pemberton had dug in along the south bank of the Yalobusha River. Rain fell in torrents and turned the roads into ribbons of mud in which the soldiers sank to their knees and wagons were mired axle deep. Although Grant detached troops to guard his ever lengthening supply and communications lines, the lines remained exposed and vulnerable.

On December 20, raiding Confederate cavalry under Major General Earl Van Dorn captured the Federal supply base at Holly Springs and destroyed mountains of supplies. The Mobile & Ohio Railroad, on which Grant depended for supplies, also fell prey to the Confederate raiders of Brigadier General Nathan Bedford Forrest. The destruction of the vital rail line and his advance base at Holly Springs compelled Grant to pull back to Memphis. Placing his men on half rations, the Federal commander was forced to accept temporary defeat and search for a more promising route to Vicksburg.

On the same day as the Confederate raid on Holly Springs, the lead elements of Sherman's Expeditionary Force boarded transports at Memphis and headed down river toward Vicksburg. The next day, Sherman learned of the disaster at Holly Springs but continued the movement toward the "Hill City." The operation now become a race to see which force would reach Vicksburg first—Sherman's, moving by water, or Pemberton's, moving from Grenada via interior rail lines. It was a race Sherman would lose.

To pave the way for Sherman's landing near Chickasaw

Bayou, north of Vicksburg, Lieutenant Commander Thomas O. Selfridge, Jr. led a flotilla, consisting of the ironclad *Cairo*, her sister ship *Pittsburg*, and several smaller vessels up the Yazoo River to clear the channel of torpedoes (mines). As the flotilla approached Drumgould's Bluff on the morning of December 12, 1862, sailors spotted several torpedoes. A skiff was lowered and sailors attempted to clear the torpedoes, while riflemen on the bows of the vessels shot at others in the hope of detonating them before they came into proximity. Hearing small arms fire, and fearing that his flotilla was under attack, Selfridge ordered the smaller vessels out of the way and pushed *Cairo* into the lead, intending to shell the banks and drive off the sharpshooters. Just as his vessel took the lead it

JOHN C. PEMBERTON

Born Pennsylvania 1814; privately educated, Pemberton shunned his Quaker ancestry to attend the U.S. Military Academy, graduating in 1837, twenty-seventh in his class of fifty; commissioned a 2d lieutenant in the 4th Artillery, he saw action against the Seminoles in Florida; promoted to 1st lieutenant in 1842, he was posted to Fortress Monroe; while at Norfolk he married into a prominent local family; as an artillerist and later as an aide-de-camp to General W.J. Worth during the Mexican War, he was twice wounded and earned brevets to captain and major; promoted to captain in 1850, he served on the frontier and participated in the 1958 Mormon Expedition; as the secession crisis erupted into war, Pemberton resigned his commission, declining General Winfield Scott's offer of colonelcy in the U.S. forces; he tendered his services to Virginia, becoming a lieutenant colonel in the state's provisional army in April 1861; only days later he was elevated to colonel and charged with training new cavalry and artillery units; Pemberton entered

was rocked by two loud explosions. In a matter of minutes *Cairo* was on the bottom in six fathoms of water, the first victim in naval history of an electrically detonated torpedo. Incredibly, no lives were lost when *Cairo* went down, and the loss of the powerful ironclad did nothing to deter Sherman's movement. (*Cairo* sat on the bottom for almost one hundred years before her resting place was discovered by National Park Service historian Edwin C. Bearss in 1956. Salvage operations commenced three years later and were completed in 1964 when on December 12—102 years after she sank—*Cairo* was brought to the surface. The boat has since been restored and is on display in Vicksburg National Military Park.)

Christmas Eve found the ranking officers of the Vicksburg

Confederate service as a major of artillery in June, but was quickly appointed brigadier general; after commanding a brigade at Norfolk, he was promoted to major general to rank from January 1862, commanding the Department of South Carolina, Georgia, and Florida; promoted to lieutenant general in October 1862, he took command of the Department of Mississippi and East Louisiana; his primary task was to maintain control of the Mississippi at Vicksburg; ordered to defend the city at all costs, he was outmatched by General U.S. Grant's Federal forces in a series battles and forced into Vicksburg's defenses to stand a siege; with his army and the remaining citizenry starving, and with no hope of relief, Pemberton surrendered the city and its garrison on July 4, 1863; Southerners demanded a scapegoat, and the Northern-born general offered an easy target for unfounded accusations of treason; exchanged but disgraced, Pemberton was left without a command commensurate with his rank; despite his disappointment and the criticism he endured, he remained loyal to the Confederate cause; resigning his lieutenant general's commission in May 1864, he vowed to continue the fight as a private, but a sympathetic President Jefferson Davis appointed his friend a lieutenant colonel of artillery, and as such Pemberton served faithfully for the remainder of the war; after the war he farmed in Virginia, but in 1875 he moved to Philadelphia, where he died in 1881.

garrison at a gala ball hosted by Dr. William Balfour and his wife Emma. As the Southern officers and belles of Vicksburg, resplendent in their finest gowns, danced the night away, they were unaware of the Federal fleet's approach and revelled in a false sense of security. Upstream, at Point Lookout, eleven miles below Lake Providence, Louisiana, two Confederates manned a lonely telegraph station. Suddenly, a young black girl rushed into the room to inform the soldiers that there were several boats on the river; she implored the soldiers to take a look. Stumbling through the darkness to the river bank, the

EARL VAN DORN

Born Mississippi 1820; Van Dorn was graduated from the U.S. Military Academy in 1842, fifty-second in his class of fifty-six; a brevet second lieutenant, he was posted to the 7th Infantry; he owned an exceptionally active career, serving in various garrison and frontier commands; twice brevetted for the Mexican War, he was promoted to first lieutenant in 1847 and served against the Seminoles in Florida; in 1855 Van Dorn became a captain in the newly organized 2d U.S. Cavalry, an elite regiment that included Albert Sidney Johnston, Robert E. Lee, George H. Thomas, William J. Hardee, and John B. Hood; in Texas he fought numerous actions against the Comanches and was wounded in an engagement in Indian Territory; with Mississippi's withdrawal from the Union in 1860, Van Dorn, having been promoted to major, tendered his resignation to serve his native state; he became a brigadier general of Mississippi state troops and rose to major general commanding state troops upon Jefferson Davis's election as president of the Confederate States; entering Confederate service in March 1861, Van Dorn was commissioned a colonel and briefly commanded Forts Jackson and St. Philip that guarded the southern approaches to New Orleans; he was soon appointed commander of the Department of Texas,

two men could make out huge dark shapes on the water and recognized them as Union gunboats and transports, loaded to the gunwales with troops headed for Vicksburg. The squadron, which numbered seven gunboats and fifty-nine transports, had reached Milliken's Bend, Louisiana, just above Vicksburg, and tied-up for the night. Without a moment to lose, the soldiers hurried to sound the alarm.

Returning to their telegraph station, the two men frantically sent the signal over the wires to De Soto Point, opposite Vicksburg, where the message was deciphered by Philip Fall.

where his performance earned him promotion to brigadier general in June 1861; ordered to Virginia, he was elevated to major general and commanded a division under General Joseph E. Johnston; returned to the West in January 1862, he commanded the Trans-Mississippi District of Department Number Two and the small Army of the West; that March he was defeated at the Battle of Pea Ridge; he then led his army across the Mississippi to reinforce General P.G.T. Beauregard's beleaguered force at Corinth, Mississippi; given command of the Department of Southern Mississippi and East Louisiana, he worked to defend Vicksburg, but his harsh administration of the department led to his removal in July 1862; after being soundly defeated at Corinth in October, he assumed command of the cavalry under his successor in Mississippi, General John C. Pemberton; much better suited for a cavalry command, Van Dorn turned in his finest Civil War performance with his December 1862 raid on General U.S. Grant's Holly Springs depot; in addition to destroying tons of Federal supplies, the raid delayed Grant's advance on Vicksburg; Van Dorn then headed a cavalry division in General Braxton Bragg's Army of Tennessee and was successful in several clashes in central Tennessee; a handsome and dashing figure, Van Dorn, although married, was a known ladies' man, whose transgressions often drew the consternation of fellow officers and citizens alike; while headquartered at Spring Hill, Tennessee, he spent much time with the young wife of a local physician; in May 1863 the aggrieved husband, Dr. James Peters, confronted Van Dorn in the general's quarters and shot him to death.

Understanding the importance of the message, Fall jumped into a skiff and rowed across the Mississippi River, landing at the base of the Vicksburg bluffs. Running up the hill, the courier raced through quiet streets to the Balfour house. As the officers danced with their ladies, Fall pushed his way through the crowd to inform Major General Martin Luther Smith, commander of the Vicksburg garrison, that the enemy was approaching the city. Smith exclaimed, "This ball is at an end; the enemy are coming down the river, all non-combatants must leave the city." The troops were called to arms and prepared to do battle with Sherman.

The field of battle would be north of the city, fronting the Walnut Hills. Along the base of the hills the Confederates established a formidable line of defense that throughout most of its length was shielded by water barriers. They also felled trees in front of their works, forming a dense obstruction to any Union advance. Although the Confederates were greatly outnumbered, their fortifications were strong, and reinforcements were on the way from northern Mississippi.

Following a Christmas repast of hardtack and coffee, Sherman's force came ashore on December 26 and 27, moving cautiously inland until they were fired upon by Confederates posted in the woods along Chickasaw Bayou. The fighting escalated on December 27 and 28 as the Federals probed for an opening in the Confederate defenses. During this two-day period Sherman altered and solidified the disposition of his troops. The Confederates, now under the personal command of General Pemberton, strengthened their position, while several thousand additional troops moved into line.

At 7:30 a.m. on December 29 Union artillery roared into action. Confederate cannoneers responded, initiating an artillery duel that lasted for several hours but did little damage to either side. Union officers reconnoitered and at 11 o'clock began to deploy their troops in line of battle. Before them was a formidable task and the chances of success were slim. General Sherman himself admitted the difficult nature of the situation: "We will lose 5,000 men before we take Vicksburg, and may as well lose them here as anywhere else." When the attack was ordered at noon, Colonel John F. DeCourcy, whose troops would spearhead the assault, lamented, "My poor brigade!"

At twelve o'clock Sherman's artillery fired the signal volley to begin the attack. Blue-clad soldiers of DeCourcy's and Brigadier General Frank Blair's Brigades surged forward with a cheer. Braving a storm of shells and minié balls, DeCourcy's troops suffered heavy casualties in crossing a narrow causeway that spanned Chickasaw Bayou but carried the advance Confederate rifle-pits. The 4th Iowa was the only regiment of Brigadier General John M. Thayer's Brigade to follow DeCourcy's men across the bayou, forming on DeCourcy's right. As the Federals closed on the main Confederate line, they were checked by a murderous fire and driven back with frightful losses. The remnants of Blair's and DeCourcy's Brigades, as well as the 4th Iowa, fell back across Chickasaw Bayou via a corduroy bridge, having done more than could be reasonably expected of mortal men.

Confederate Brigadier General Stephen D. Lee, whose troops had checked the Federal attack in this sector, seized the opportunity to launch a counterattack. The 17th and 26th Louisiana Infantry Regiments moved forward, capturing 21 officers and 311 enlisted men, 4 battle flags, and 500 stands of arms. The Confederates had dealt a decisive repulse to Sherman's main assault and they repeated the performance elsewhere along the line.

As darkness enveloped the fields, a hard, cold rain began to fall and continued throughout the night. Fires were not permitted, and Union and Confederate soldiers alike suffered from exposure. A Federal infantryman from Missouri later wrote, "The rain did not stop until morning—the storm raging with unbroken fury, and when daylight at last dawned upon the pitiful scene we found ourselves...stiff blue and teeth rattling, scarcely able to walk, and many totally unable to speak."

Unwilling to accept defeat so easily, Sherman contemplated an assault against the Confederate works at Snyder's Bluff, farther upstream. The weather, however, was against him as a dense fog blanketed the area. Sherman knew that an assault under such conditions would be difficult and attended with a "fearful sacrifice of life." Reluctantly, he ordered his troops back to the Yazoo River, where they embarked on transports and returned to Milliken's Bend to await instructions from Grant. The operations at Chickasaw Bayou had cost the Federals 1,776 casualties: 208 were killed; 1,005 wounded; and 563 missing. Confederate losses totaled only 187 men. In reporting the action, Sherman simply wrote, "I reached Vicksburg at the time appointed, landed, assaulted and failed."

Although his first effort to scale the mountain had met with failure, Grant was undaunted as he returned to Memphis to contemplate his next move against Vicksburg.

3
FRUSTRATION AND FAILURE

Sherman's hasty, perhaps ill-advised, departure from Memphis on December 20 that ended with his bloody repulse near Vicksburg nine days later was partly in response to rumors that he was to be superseded in command of the expedition. While he and Grant planned their campaign, Major General John A. McClernand, a former Democratic member of Congress from Illinois, was given authority by President Lincoln to command the Mississippi River expedition. Prior to leaving Illinois, however, the general took time to get married. The honeymooners traveled south to Memphis only to learn that the troops McClernand was to command had been commandeered by Sherman and led to defeat on the banks of Chickasaw Bayou.

Energetic, aggressive, and ambitious, McClernand was also bombastic, egotistical, and extremely irritating to those around him. Born in Kentucky, he was raised in Illinois and

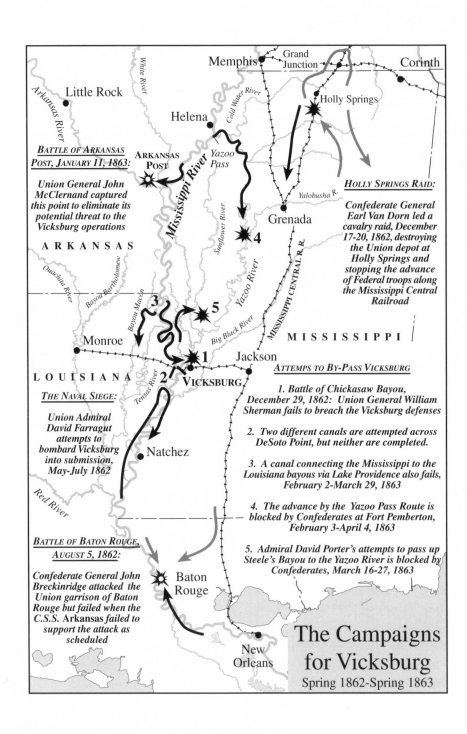

The Campaigns for Vicksburg
Spring 1862-Spring 1863

BATTLE OF ARKANSAS POST, JANUARY 11, 1863:

Union General John McClernand captured this point to eliminate its potential threat to the Vicksburg operations

HOLLY SPRINGS RAID:

Confederate General Earl Van Dorn led a cavalry raid, December 17-20, 1862, destroying the Union depot at Holly Springs and stopping the advance of Federal troops along the Mississippi Central Railroad

ATTEMPS TO BY-PASS VICKSBURG

1. Battle of Chickasaw Bayou, December 29, 1862: Union General William Sherman fails to breach the Vicksburg defenses

2. Two different canals are attempted across DeSoto Point, but neither are completed.

3. A canal connecting the Mississippi to the Louisiana bayous via Lake Providence also fails, February 2-March 29, 1863

4. The advance by the Yazoo Pass Route is blocked by Confederates at Fort Pemberton, February 3-April 4, 1863

5. Admiral David Porter's attempts to pass up Steele's Bayou to the Yazoo River is blocked by Confederates, March 16-27, 1863

THE NAVAL SIEGE:

Union Admiral David Farragut attempts to bombard Vicksburg into submission, May-July 1862

BATTLE OF BATON ROUGE, AUGUST 5, 1862:

Confederate General John Breckinridge attacked the Union garrison of Baton Rouge but failed when the C.S.S. Arkansas failed to support the attack as scheduled

had a strong dislike for abolitionists. He was short, spare of frame, and heavily bearded with a rather large nose and scraggly hair. He had piercing eyes, a hearty laugh, and an engaging smile, yet at all times was calculating and deceitful. A lawyer by training and a politician by profession, McClernand had risen to the pinnacle of power in the House of Representatives only to be defeated for the speakership in 1860. He looked to the field of battle to win victories and headlines in his quest for the White House.

Rushing to the vicinity of Vicksburg, McClernand assumed command of Federal forces at Milliken's Bend on January 4, 1863, and christened them the Army of the Mississippi. Anxious for action, he embraced Sherman's recommendation to seize Arkansas Post, a place 50 miles up the Arkansas River from which the Confederates could send gunboats into the Mississippi. Moving with remarkable speed, McClernand's force reached its objective on January 9th and two days later forced the surrender of Fort Hindman and almost 5,000 Rebel soldiers. Although the victory secured headlines for McClernand at a time when the North was desperate for good news, his victory was downplayed by Grant, who said it was not the proper theater of operations and termed it "a wild goose chase," that is until he found out that his friend Sherman had recommended the campaign. In all fairness to McClernand, his actions eliminated a major threat to Union operations on the Mississippi River and a potential source of trouble for Grant's future operations in Louisiana and Mississippi.

Checked on the overland route, Grant seized upon Federal naval supremacy on the inland waters to transfer his Army of the Tennessee to Milliken's Bend and to Young's Point, Louisiana, on the Mississippi River just north of and opposite Vicksburg. He also stationed troops farther to the north at Lake Providence, Louisiana. On January 30, 1863, shortly after his arrival at the front, Grant issued General Orders No.

13, in which he announced, "I hereby assume immediate command of the expedition against Vicksburg, and department headquarters will hereafter be with the expedition." (By this action, McClernand's authority was limited to that of the XIII Corps, Army of the Tennessee.)

During the winter months, as Grant marshaled his forces in Louisiana, his troops stockpiled tremendous quantities of rations, clothing, medicine, ammunition, and countless other items in preparation for the spring campaign against Vicksburg. "The water was high and the rains were incessant," recorded Grant. "There seemed no possibility of a land move-

JOHN A. McCLERNAND

Born Kentucky 1812; as a child, McClernand moved with his family to Illinois; he studied law and was admitted to the bar in 1832, but other interests kept him from practicing; he fought in the Black Hawk War and edited a newspaper before entering the state assembly in 1836, serving until 1843, when he took a seat in the U.S. House of Representatives as a Democrat; a fine orator, he served a total of five terms in the House (1843-1851 and 1859-1861), taking

an active part in the Compromise of 1850; although he possessed a fierce dislike for abolitionists, he was nonetheless unwavering in his support of the Union; with the onset of the Civil War, McClernand's efforts to rally support and recruit troops for the Federal army proved invaluable; recognizing McClernand's political value, President Lincoln appointed him brigadier general of U.S. Volunteers in August 1861; that October he resigned his seat in Congress to command a brigade in Missouri and southern Illinois, participating in the Battle of Belmont; in February 1862 McClernand took command of a division in the Army of the Tennessee, and was promoted to major general of Volunteers in March; he saw action at Fort Donelson, Shiloh, and Corinth, leav-

ment before the end of March or later, and it would not do to lie idle all this time. The effect would be demoralizing to the troops and injurious to their health."

In an effort to keep his troops busy and the spirit of the offensive alive, the Union commander orchestrated a series of ill-fated bayou expeditions, the object of which was to reach the rear of Vicksburg. Grant termed them "experiments" and wrote that his purpose was "to consume time, and to divert the attention of the enemy, of my troops, and of the public generally." Although many of his subordinates expressed confidence in these operations, the army commander did not share their

ing the army in October to recruit a new army, which he would command in a move against Vicksburg; he successfully raised a large force, which he then forwarded to Memphis, only to have it commandeered by General W.T. Sherman for his failed attack on Chickasaw Bayou; McClernand then took command and led his short-lived Army of the Mississippi in a successful attack on Arkansas Post; shortly thereafter, his command was absorbed into General U.S. Grant's Army of the Tennessee, part of it as the Thirteenth Corps, with McClernand as commander; during the Vicksburg Campaign, McClernand angered his superiors by releasing stories to newspapers that praised the efforts of his command at the expense of the rest of the army; although he performed reasonably well in the campaign, he was relieved in June, and did not return to duty until 1864, when he again headed the Thirteenth Corps in the Department of the Gulf during the Red River Campaign; suffering from malaria, he resigned in November 1864; after the war he served as a circuit judge from 1870 to 1873 and was active in Democratic politics, chairing the party's national convention in 1876; he died at Springfield, Illinois, in 1900. Despite his self-congratulatory reports and adversarial relationships with Grant and others, McClernand made important contributions to the Union war effort, especially as a recruiter. As a combat commander, he showed certain ability, but his impact on the army in the field was largely negative. Like other political appointees, he carried from the war a deep resentment of West Point-educated professional soldiers.

optimism. "I myself never felt great confidence that any of the experiments resorted to would prove successful," he later admitted. "Nevertheless I was always prepared to take advantage of them in case they did."

Late in January, Federal forces resumed work on the canal across De Soto Point, opposite the city, that was begun the previous summer by General Williams. The canal was to be more than one mile in length, sixty feet wide, and six feet deep. Working with ax and saw, pick and shovel, the infantrymen labored to excavate the canal to the desired depth. President Lincoln was enthralled with the scheme and almost on a daily basis walked across the lawn from the White House to the War Department to inquire of Grant by telegraph, "How's work on the canal coming along?" In spite of Grant's somewhat optimistic replies, Sherman noted with candor, "The canal don't amount to much."

Although rapid progress was made, a sudden drop in the river left the bottom of the canal above the surface of the water. As the soldiers and local blacks, who had been pressed into service from nearby plantations, dug lower, there was an unexpected rise in the river that broke through the dam at the head of the canal and flooded the area. The canal began to fill with backwater and sediment. In a desperate effort to rescue the project, two huge stream-driven dipper dredges, *Hercules* and *Sampson*, were put to work clearing the channel. The dredges, however, were exposed to Confederate artillery fire from the bluffs at Vicksburg and driven away. By late March, work on the canal was abandoned.

A second canal operation was initiated in February at Lake Providence, 75-river miles above Vicksburg, as Federal engineers investigated a route that led through a 200-mile connecting chain of waterways from the lake to the mouth of Red River thence up the Mississippi River another 150 miles to Vicksburg. Based on the reports of his engineers, Grant believed that this avenue of approach "bids fair to be the most practicable route for turning Vicksburg." In early March, though, Grant personally examined the route and reported that "there was scarcely a chance of this ever becoming a practicable route for moving troops through the enemy's country."

Despite Grant's pessimistic outlook, work on the canal continued. Shortly after his visit, the levee was blasted and water from the river rushed through "with such vehemence and noise as to make one remember the falls of Niagara." Within days the proposed water route was reported to be of sufficient depth as to allow the passage of large steamboats. The route, however, was never exploited and the plan was abandoned late in March as Grant determined on an avenue of approach far more promising of success.

A third "experiment" was conducted at Yazoo Pass, 325 river miles above Vicksburg, where on February 3, 1863, the levee was breached north of Friars Point. Flood waters of the Mississippi River cascaded into Moon Lake and via Yazoo Pass rushed into the Coldwater River. Passage through these streams led to the Tallahatchie River and then into the Yazoo River, which would enable the Federals to turn Vicksburg's northern flank at Haynes' and Snyder's bluffs. Although the route was a lengthy one, once the pass was cleared of trees and logjams, it offered easy navigation for gunboats and transports.

The possibility of such a move was not lost on the Confederate officers whose troops operated in the Delta. Warnings of Federal activity at the pass were wired to Pemberton at department headquarters in Jackson. Appreciating the grave threat they implied, he ordered Major General William W. Loring to check the Federal advance. Loring moved from Yazoo City to Greenwood, where his troops and impressed slaves constructed a strong line of works composed of cotton bales and earth named Fort Pemberton. Located across a narrow neck of land between the Tallahatchie and Yazoo rivers, the fort was admirably situated for defense and there the Confederates waited for the enemy to appear.

By March 11 the Federal flotilla had worked its way through the twisting waterways to Fort Pemberton. There, the powerful ironclad *Chillicothe* opened the attack. The gunboat, however, was quickly driven off by the accurate fire of Loring's artillery. Two days later *Chillicothe*, supported by the "City Series" ironclad *De Kalb*, engaged the Confederate batteries for several hours. At the height of the exchange, Loring implored his gunners to "give them blizzards, boys." Little damage was inflicted by either side and the gunboats pulled back out of range.

Over the next several weeks, both sides rushed troops into the Delta, and Federal gunboats frequently challenged the Confederate batteries at Fort Pemberton to no avail. Sealing the fate of this expedition was the flooded countryside, which prevented the Federals from attacking with their numerically superior infantry force. Grant lamented, "It is now clearly demonstrated that a further force, in by way of Yazoo Pass, can be of no service. The party that first went in have so delayed as to give the enemy time to fortify. I see nothing for it now but to have that force return the way they went in." It took six days for the flotilla to return to Helena, Arkansas, and the Yazoo Pass Expedition came to an inglorious end.

In mid-March, as Union forces toiled on the canals and pushed through Yazoo Pass, Rear Admiral David Dixon Porter, commander of the Mississippi Squadron, recommended an alternate avenue of approach to Vicksburg. While scouting Steele's Bayou as a way to support the Yazoo Pass Expedition, Porter found that the waterways of the lower Delta provided a much shorter and, perhaps more promising, route to the Yazoo River above Snyder's Bluff. Porter hosted a reconnaissance for Grant, during which he impressed upon the general the feasibility of this route. Upon his return to army headquarters, Grant detailed troops to support the navy.

Pushing up Steele's Bayou, soldiers and sailors worked to

clear obstructions from the channel and remove low limbs that wreaked havoc with the upper decks and smokestacks of both gunboats and transport vessels. Slowly winding its way through Steele's and Black Bayous to Deer Creek, the flotilla

DAVID DIXON PORTER

Born Pennsylvania 1813; son of Commodore David Porter, he accompanied his father's pirate suppression expeditions in the Gulf of Mexico; having spent much of his early life at sea, he received little formal education; joined the Mexican Navy as a midshipman in 1827, joined U.S. Navy as midshipman in 1829; lieutenant 1841; saw considerable service during the Mexican War; served various merchant enterprises but returned to active duty in 1855; with the outbreak of Civil War, served in blockade squadrons; promoted to commander in 1861 after twenty years as a lieutenant; capably led the mortar flotilla in the capture of New Orleans; given command of the Mississippi Squadron in October 1862; for his excellent service during the Vicksburg Campaign he was elevated to rear admiral, bypassing the ranks of captain and commodore; took a large fleet up the Red River to support Major General Nathaniel P. Banks' ill-fated campaign; the fleet was harassed by Confederate land forces and slowed by low water levels during its difficult retreat; sent East, he directed the North Atlantic Squadron for the balance of the war, participating in the capture of Fort Fisher, North Carolina; superintendent of the United States Naval Academy, 1865-1869; vice admiral 1866; admiral 1870; author of numerous books including *Incidents of the Civil War* (1886) and *History of the Navy During the War of the Rebellion* (1890); he died 1891. The failure of the Red River Expedition notwithstanding, Admiral Porter played a significant role in the Federal success in the West. He was the cousin of Major General Fitz-John Porter.

neared the Rolling Fork of the Sunflower River, where the boats were stopped by trees felled into the channel as obstructions. Confederate infantry and artillery moved into position to prevent removal of the trees, while some units raced behind the fleet and felled trees to block the channel, bottling up the Union gunboats. In the gathering darkness, the Confederates moved into position along the stream bank, confident that they would capture the fleet on the morrow.

Porter, who had outdistanced his infantry support, recognized the danger he was in and scribbled a note to Sherman, imploring his assistance. The note, written on tissue paper and rolled in a tobacco leaf, was entrusted to a black man, who disappeared into the night. While he waited for help to arrive, Porter ordered the sides and decks of his vessels smeared with slime from the creek bottom to make boarding difficult. He also gave preliminary instructions to blow up the boats if necessary to prevent capture.

Tense hours passed, but when day broke on March 21 the Southerners failed to act aggressively and lost the opportunity to capture or destroy the fleet. Admiral Porter later claimed that he was on the verge of abandoning ship and destroying the flotilla when Sherman's infantrymen arrived late in the day and drove the Confederates back. Having been rescued, the fleet slowly backed down Deer Creek several miles until it reached a spot wide enough to allow the sailors to turn their boats around. Although the flotilla was saved, this "experiment," as with the others, had been a dismal failure.

Checked every way he turned, Grant was running out of time and options.

4
BOLD IS THE WARRIOR

"Sam" Grant was at a crossroads in his military career. Although he held a major field command, he continued to suffer a dubious reputation. Now, having failed in his first attempts to take Vicksburg, his future appeared tenuous at best. The Northern press clamored for his removal. Even members of the Cabinet urged Lincoln to replace Grant as commander of the Army of the Tennessee. But the president responded, "I can't spare this man, he fights. I'll try him a little longer." Cognizant of the criticism that swirled around him in both military and political circles, Grant remained stoic. Determined to persevere, he ignored his critics and remained focused on his objective—Vicksburg. After months of frustration and failure, Grant examined his remaining options.

Three alternatives were discussed at army headquarters. The first was to launch a direct amphibious assault across the Mississippi River and storm the Vicksburg stronghold. The second was to pull back to Memphis and try the overland route once again. The third was to march the army down the west side of the river, search for a favorable crossing point, and transfer the field of operations to the area south and east of Vicksburg. In characteristic fashion and with grim determination, Grant boldly opted for the march south, believing that "There was nothing left to be done but to go forward to a decisive victory." (Historian Edwin C. Bearss, writes of Grant's decision: "The third alternative was full of dangers and risks. Failure in this venture would entail little less than total destruction. If it succeeded, however, the gains would be complete and decisive.") On March 29, 1863, Grant ordered General McClernand's XIII Corps to open a road from Milliken's Bend to New Carthage on the Mississippi River below Vicksburg. The movement began on March 31. The Vicksburg campaign now began in earnest.

McClernand was a controversial selection to lead the march through Louisiana. Although an experienced fighter in the halls of Congress, his only military experience prior to the Civil War was in the Black Hawk War. As a political appointee in the military, he was inexperienced and at times inept in the handling of troops. The former congressman disdained administrative details and was contemptuous of military protocol. He did not work well with superiors or subordinates and his hatred for West Pointers did not endear him to his fellow corps commanders—Sherman and Major General James B. McPherson. But McClernand had demonstrated his willingness to fight at Fort Donelson and Shiloh and had developed into an able combat officer. Although Grant knew of widespread distrust of McClernand and later wrote that he "doubted McClernand's fitness," in the spring of 1863 Grant was confident that the former congressman could and, if necessary, would fight.

On March 31 a task force commanded by Colonel Thomas W. Bennett of the 69th Indiana Infantry left its encampment at

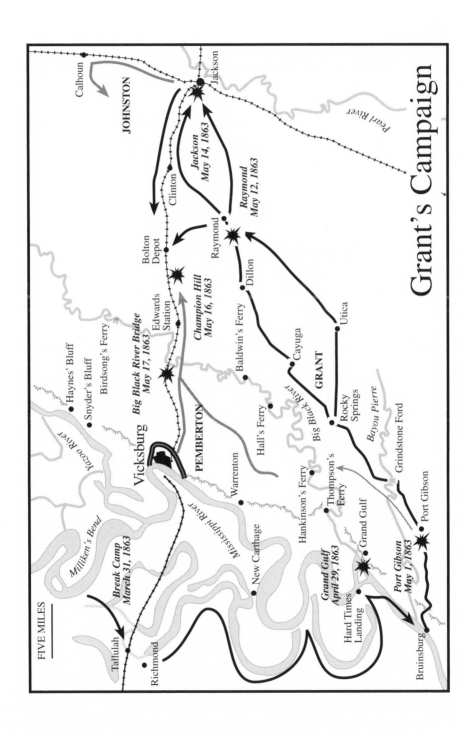

Grant's Campaign

John S. Bowen

Born Georgia 1830; Bowen received his early education in Georgia and entered the U.S. Military Academy in 1848 with the class of 1852; although an excellent cadet, he was court-martialed and expelled for his failure to report a fellow cadet's unauthorized absence; President Millard Fillmore lessened the penalty to a one year suspension, and Bowen graduated thirteenth of fifty-two in the outstanding class of 1853, which included future Civil War generals J.B. Hood, Philip Sheridan, J.B. McPherson, and John Schofield, among others; breveted 2d lieutenant and assigned to the Mounted Rifles, Bowen served at Jefferson Barracks, Missouri, and on the Texas-Mexico bor-

der; he resigned his commission in 1856 to be an architect in Savannah, but soon relocated to St. Louis, where he became an officer in the state militia; with pro-secession forces at Camp Jackson in May 1861, he was captured and paroled, agreeing not to take up arms against the United States until exchanged; this he soon violated, raising a regiment of Missourians that entered Confederate service as the 1st Missouri Infantry, with Bowen as its colonel; he held various commands in Kentucky and Missouri before gaining promotion to brigadier general in March 1862; at Shiloh in April, he was wounded while leading a brigade in heavy fighting; returning to duty, he served under General Earl Van Dorn in Mississippi; Bowen played a major role in the 1863 defense of Vicksburg; commanding a division, he held Grand Gulf on April 29, and two days later fought a stubborn all-day battle before yielding Port Gibson; he also fought well in the Confederate loss at Champion Hill on May 16, but the next day his outnumbered division was routed at Big Black River Bridge; promoted to major general on May 25, Bowen performed splendidly throughout the Siege of Vicksburg and, although ravaged by dysentery, helped to arrange the July 4 surrender; paroled and awaiting exchange, his health steadily worsened; he died near Edwards, Mississippi, less than two weeks after the fall of Vicksburg. A capable officer who demonstrated flashes of excellence in combat, General Bowen would be missed in the Confederacy's leadership-strapped western armies.

Milliken's Bend with instructions to reconnoiter the road to New Carthage. Informed that the road was passable, the ever-eager McClernand dispatched additional troops to make necessary repairs. Over the next several days the entire XIII Corps took up the line of march, slogging its way south over muddy roads. The troops marched down the west side of the river

FRANCIS MARION COCKRELL

Born Missouri 1834; Cockrell studied law and passed the bar in 1855; at the outbreak of the Civil War, he worked on behalf of pro-secession forces in his native state, raising a company for the Missouri State Guard, with which he saw action at Carthage and Wilson's Creek; entering Confederate service as captain in the 2d Missouri Infantry, he fought at Pea Ridge in March 1862; elevated to lieutenant colonel in May and colonel in June, he led the 2d Missouri at Corinth in October 1862; during the defense of Vicksburg, he led a brigade in General John Bowen's Division, seeing action at Grand Gulf, Port Gibson, Big Black River Bridge, and Champion Hill; surrendered and paroled with the Vicksburg garrison on July 4, 1863, Cockrell was not exchanged until September, having been promoted to brigadier general in July; returning to duty, he commanded a brigade in General Leonidas Polk's Army of Mississippi (later General A.P. Stewart's Corps, Army of Tennessee), which he led through most of the Atlanta Campaign; during General J.B. Hood's disastrous Tennessee Campaign, Cockrell was severely wounded in the bloody attack at Franklin; after recovering, he led troops in the defense of Mobile, where he was captured in April 1865; after the war, the practiced law in Missouri; in 1874 he was elected to the first of five terms (serving 30 years) in the US Senate; leaving the Senate in 1905, he was named to the Interstate Commerce Commission; General Cockrell died at Washington, D.C., in 1915.

along natural levees, building bridges and corduroying roads almost every step of the way. Progress was slow and the work back-breaking, but by mid-April McClernand secured New Carthage for use as a forward staging area.

A movement by such large numbers of troops was difficult to conceal from the eyes of roving Confederate cavalry. Rumors of the Federal advance reached the ears of Brigadier General John S. Bowen, Confederate commander at Grand Gulf, twenty-five miles below Vicksburg. Bowen reacted instinctively when the rumors were confirmed. On April 4 he sent Colonel Francis M. Cockrell across the river to make contact with the enemy. Ordered to keep his superior apprised of enemy movements, Cockrell crossed the river with the 1st and 2nd Missouri Infantry Regiments and a section of artillery. Quickly making contact with the head of McClernand's column, the aggressive colonel sent Bowen frequent and fairly accurate reports of Federal movements. Bowen, in turn, notified departmental headquarters in Jackson of the developing threat and braced himself to meet the Union onslaught should it be aimed at Grand Gulf.

As Grant's infantrymen pushed southward through Louisiana, Admiral Porter's fleet prepared to run by the batteries at Vicksburg. On the dark, moonless night of April 16 Porter's crews raised anchor and moved their vessels downriver toward the citadel—with engines muffled and running lights extinguished. Porter hoped to slip past the batteries undetected, but his hopes were dashed. As the boats rounded De Soto Point, above Vicksburg, they were spotted by Confederate lookouts, who spread the alarm. Suddenly the night sky was ablaze from bales of cotton soaked in turpentine that lined the river on both banks and barrels of tar set afire by the Southerners to illuminate the river and silhouette the fleet as it passed the batteries.

For several hours the fleet withstood the punishing fire that poured from Confederate batteries. Admiral Porter paid close attention to where the shot and shell struck his vessels and noticed that they had hit smokestacks, pilothouses, and hurricane decks. Some even hit the gundecks, but few hit any lower, where the vital parts of his boats—engines, boilers, steamdrums, and mud filters—were located. He reasoned that there was a fatal flaw in the placement of Confederate batteries that did not allow the guns to be depressed for a more effective fire.

The admiral quickly ordered his captains to move their vessels across the channel—to hug the Mississippi shore. As they did so, the shot and shell began to fly harmlessly overhead. The fleet came so close to Vicksburg that sailors reportedly heard Confederate gun captains issue commands. They also heard bricks tumble into the city streets, the effect of their own gunfire. When the shelling stopped, Porter tallied the damage to his fleet and recorded the loss of only one transport vessel. What many deemed impossible had now been achieved. With a portion of the fleet now below Vicksburg, Grant had the wherewithal to cross the mighty river.

By the end of April the XIII Corps and two divisions of the XVII Corps, along with Porter's gunboats, were concentrated at Hard Times Landing, poised for a strike across the Mississippi. Grant intended to force a crossing of the river at Grand Gulf, where there was a good all weather landing and from which point roads radiated deep into the interior of Mississippi. Once ashore the Federals would move on fortress Vicksburg from the south.

To increase the chances of success for the planned crossing at Grand Gulf, Grant had earlier in the month ordered a series of diversionary cavalry raids. These raids were designed not only to sever Vicksburg's vital supply and communications lines, but to confuse Pemberton and keep him off-balance. The most successful of these raids was led by Colonel Benjamin H. Grierson, whose hard riding troopers raced the length of Mississippi from La Grange, Tennessee, to Baton Rouge, Louisiana, destroying railroads and telegraph lines.

Bombarded with reports of enemy movements throughout his department and pleas for reinforcements, Pemberton acted in characteristic fashion—indecisively. In a futile attempt to capture Grierson, he weakened his strategic river defenses and scattered his available manpower.

To be prepared should the raids fail, Grant also ordered the XV Corps to make a demonstration toward Snyder's Bluff in order to prevent the movement of Confederate reinforcements from Vicksburg to Grand Gulf. The XV Corps, which was still encamped at Milliken's Bend and Young's Point, was commanded by Grant's most trusted and experienced subordinate— Sherman. The demonstration, made from April 29 to May 1 in

BENJAMIN H. GRIERSON

Born Pennsylvania 1826; Grierson taught music in Ohio and Illinois, and for a time worked as a merchant; at the outbreak of the Civil War he served as a volunteer aide-de-camp to Federal General Benjamin Prentiss; commissioned a major in the 6th Illinois Cavalry in October 1861 and promoted to colonel the following April, he served in Tennessee and Mississippi; he held a succession of brigade commands in the Army of the Tennessee from November 1862 to June 1863; from April 17 to May 2, 1863, Grierson led one of the most spectacular and successful raids of the Civil War; with a brigade of three cavalry regiments and a battery of artillery, he rode across Mississippi, from La Grange, Tennessee, to Baton Rouge, Louisiana, to draw attention away from General U.S. Grant's Vicksburg operations, capturing some 500 Confederate soldiers, 1000 horses and mules, and tons of arms and supplies, while destroying miles of railroad track, all at small loss to the Federals; Grant called the raid "one of the brilliant cavalry exploits of the war." Grierson was rewarded with promotion to brigadier general of U.S. Volunteers and assigned

conjunction with naval forces on the Yazoo River, was a feeble effort that made little impression on the Confederates.

Fortunately for Grant, Pemberton and many of his subordinates continued to believe that the Federal movement against Vicksburg would be launched north of the city. Even though most of Porter's fleet was below Vicksburg, Sherman's demonstration served to strengthen this belief. So firm were Pemberton's expectations that reports from Grand Gulf, which detailed the Federal movements in Louisiana, were not taken seriously until the situation became critical.

By April 28, Bowen considered the situation to be just that—critical. From his lookout atop Point of Rocks, above

to command a cavalry brigade in the Nineteenth Corps, Department of the Gulf; in July 1863 he took command of a cavalry division in the Sixteenth Corps, Army of the Tennessee, with which he took part in the Meridian Campaign; in June 1864, as commander of the Cavalry Corps, District of West Tennessee, he led part of the Federal force that was routed by General N.B. Forrest's Confederates at Brice's Cross Roads; later in 1864, Grierson conducted a series of successful raids in Tennessee and Mississippi; he spent the balance of the war on duty in western Tennessee; in 1865 he received brevets to major general of Volunteers and through major general in the regular establishment; promoted to major general of Volunteers in March 1866 to rank from the previous May, he mustered out of the Volunteers in April 1866; offered a regular commission, he became colonel of the 10th Cavalry, one of two newly authorized mounted regiments comprised of black troopers and white officers; for more than twenty years Grierson and his "Buffalo Soldiers" served faithfully, mostly against Indians on the fronteer, and often under the most difficult conditions; promoted to the regular rank of brigadier general in 1890, he retired the same year; he died at Omena, Michigan, in 1911; the music teacher-turned-soldier, Grierson overcame a life-long fear of horses (he had once been kicked in the face and left blemished for life) to become a truly fine cavalry officer. His 1863 raid inspired a motion picture *The Horse Soldiers*, starring John Wayne and William Holden.

Grand Gulf, Bowen watched in awe as the invasion armada prepared for action. He informed Pemberton of these dramatic developments and requested "that every man and gun that can be spared from other points be sent here." His plea was largely ignored, and Bowen was left to his own devices for the defense of Grand Gulf.

To Bowen's good fortune, his fortifications were strong. Situated forty feet above the river, dug into the side of Point of Rocks, was Fort Cobun. Protected by a parapet nearly forty feet thick, the fort contained four large guns manned by Company A, 1st Louisiana Heavy Artillery. A double line of rifle-pits and a covered way led south from Cobun three-quarters of a mile to Fort Wade. The lower fort, erected above the fire-gutted town, was on a shelf twenty feet above the muddy Mississippi. Fort Wade contained four large guns and several light field pieces manned by the skilled artillerists of Captain Henry Guibor's and Colonel William Wade's Missouri batteries. Bowen was determined to check the powerful force gathered opposite his batteries at Hard Times and prepared the Grand Gulf garrison for battle.

At 7 a.m. on April 29 the Union fleet pulled away from Hard Times Landing and steamed into action. Seven gunboats, including "City Series" ironclads *Carondelet, Louisville, Mound City,* and *Pittsburg,* each mounting thirteen guns, bombarded the Grand Gulf defenses for five hours in an attempt to silence the Confederate cannon and clear the way for a landing by Federal infantry. From the deck of a small tug, Grant watched as the battle opened. Thick clouds of white-blue smoke soon obscured his vision, yet the sheets of flame which pierced the smoke evidenced the magnitude of resistance. Hours slowly passed and the chances of success dimmed. But Grant maintained his composure. With the ever-present stub of a cigar clenched in his teeth and field glasses in hand, he kept his eyes fixed on the bluffs that towered over the opposite shore.

The bombardment raged in unabated fury throughout the

morning hours. The powerful ironclads hammered away at the earthen forts, sending solid shot and shell crashing among the Confederate defenders. Included among the casualties was Colonel Wade, who was decapitated. Although Porter's guns silenced Fort Wade, his fleet failed to quiet the fire from Fort Cobun. In the exchange of fire with Bowen's batteries, the gunboats were hit repeatedly and the fleet sustained heavy damage. Aboard the flagship *Benton*, seven men were killed and nineteen wounded; *Pittsburg* reported the loss of six killed and thirteen wounded; and *Tuscumbia*, hit 81 times, suffered the loss of five killed and twenty-four wounded. Total casualties reported by Admiral Porter were 18 killed and 57 wounded. Confederate casualties were light in comparison, only 3 killed and 19 wounded. Bitterly disappointed, Porter was forced to disengage, declaring that "Grand Gulf is the strongest place on the Mississippi."

Not wishing to send his transports loaded to the gunwales with troops to attempt a landing in the face of enemy fire, Grant, ever adaptive, disembarked his men and marched them five miles farther south along the levee at the base of Coffee Point. That evening, Porter's fleet ran past the Confederate batteries and rendezvoused with Grant at Disharoon's plantation. From April 30 to May 1 Grant pushed his army across the mighty river and onto Mississippi soil at Bruinsburg. A band aboard the flagship *Benton* struck up "The Red, White, and Blue" as Grant's infantrymen came ashore unopposed. In one of the largest amphibious operations in American history to that time, Grant landed 24,000 men to begin the inland campaign to capture Vicksburg. The Union commander later wrote:

> When this was effected I felt a degree of relief
> scarcely ever equalled since. Vicksburg was
> not yet taken it is true, nor were its defenders
> demoralized by any of the previous moves. I
> was now in the enemy's country, with a vast

river and the stronghold of Vicksburg between
me and my base of supplies. But I was on dry
ground on the same side of the river with the
enemy. All the campaigns, labors, hardships
and exposures from the month of December
previous to this time that had been made and
endured, were for the accomplishment of this
one objective.

After months of maneuver, the Army of the Tennessee was
finally on dry ground east of the Mississippi River. Although
many bloody fields of battle lay between them and Vicksburg,
the soldiers took up the line of march with firmness of purpose
and buoyant spirits.

5
THE INLAND CAMPAIGN BEGINS

Once ashore in Mississippi, Grant's forces pushed rapidly inland and took possession of the bluffs, thereby securing the landing area. By late afternoon on April 30, 16,000 men were ashore and the march inland began. The march was a difficult one for soldiers laden with sixty rounds of ammunition and more rations than could be carried in their haversacks. First Lieutenant Samuel C. Jones of Company A, 22d Iowa Infantry, recorded the method by which extra rations were carried: "The bayonets were placed on their guns and run through the meat, so each man had his extra ration of meat fixed on his bayonet. Then at a right shoulder shift, we proceeded on our march." Men of other units did the same and, as Lieutenant Jones observed, "the whole army could be seen for miles, worming its way over that vast flat country with the bayonets gleaming in the sunshine, and the ration of meat in its place. It was picturesque and beautiful to behold."

The soldiers reached the top of the bluffs, where a magnificent panorama opened before their eyes. Off to their left, amidst vast fields of corn, was Windsor, one of the largest and most ornate mansions in the South. Built by Smith Coffee Daniell, II, Windsor epitomized the opulence associated with Southern aristocracy. General McClernand established his headquarters at the mansion while many Union soldiers rested in the shade of stately oaks. At Windsor, McClernand made the decision to push on by a forced march that night, hoping to secure the bridges across Big and Little Bayou Pierre at Port Gibson. The march was resumed at 5:30 p.m.

Instead of taking the Bruinsburg Road, which was the direct road from the landing area to Port Gibson, the Union column marched south to Bethel Church, where the men turned left onto the Rodney-Port Gibson Road. Darkness soon settled over the fields and scattered forest and the pace of the march slowed to a crawl. First Sergeant Charles A. Hobbs of the 99th Illinois recorded his experience that night:

> As we pass along an old darkey gives us his blessings, but fears there will be few of us ever to return. The moon is shining above us and the road is romantic in the extreme. The artillery wagons rattle forward and the heavy tramp of many men gives a dull but impressive sound.
>
> In many places the road seems to end abruptly, but when we come to the place we find it turning at right angles, passing through narrow valleys, sometimes through hills, and presenting the best opportunity to the Rebels for defense if they had but known our purpose.

Back at Grand Gulf, General Bowen had watched helplessly as the Union fleet passed his batteries on the evening of April

29. The fiery Missourian moved quickly to redeploy his men and counter the Federal threat to his downstream flank. Knowing that he was almost powerless to contest a crossing of the river without massive reinforcements, Bowen directed two brigades into the woods west of Port Gibson. Brigadier General Martin E. Green's Brigade of Mississippians and Arkansans took position astride the Rodney Road near Magnolia Church, while Brigadier General Edward D. Tracy's Alabama Brigade, recent arrivals from Vicksburg, formed a line of battle athwart the Bruinsburg Road. The two wings were widely separated by the densely wooded valley of Centers Creek, but terrain favored the defenders. The Confederates settled down for the night in full expectation of meeting the enemy in the morning.

Hours passed slowly and tensions mounted on both sides as the inevitable clash neared. Shortly after midnight on May 1 the ever-vigilant Martin Green rode forward to see that his pickets were alert. Riding into the yard at the A.K. Shaifer house on the Rodney Road, Green was amused to see the women of the house frantically loading a wagon with all their household items. The general tried to calm their fears, telling them that the enemy could not possibly arrive before daylight. Just then, the crash of musketry shattered the stillness and several bullets struck the wagon-load of furniture. Contrary to Green's assurances the Federals had arrived. The terrified women, screaming with fright, leaped into the wagon and whipped the animals toward Port Gibson.

At the sound of firing, soldiers in blue and gray sprang into motion. The vanguard of the Federal column immediately deployed for battle and artillery batteries moved forward, dropped trail, and roared into action. A spirited skirmish ensued that lasted until 3 a.m. The Confederates held their ground, and for the next several hours an uneasy calm settled over the woods and fields as soldiers of both armies rested on their arms. Throughout the night Federal officers gathered their forces in hand as both sides prepared for the battle that they knew would resume with the rising sun.

At dawn Union troops began to move in force along the Rodney Road toward Magnolia Church. McClernand, as senior officer on the field, also directed one division to advance over a connecting plantation road on his left, toward the Bruinsburg Road along which Tracy's Alabamians could be seen in force. With skirmishers well in advance, the Federals began a slow and deliberate advance at about 5:30 a.m. The Confederates contested the advance on both fronts and the battle began in earnest.

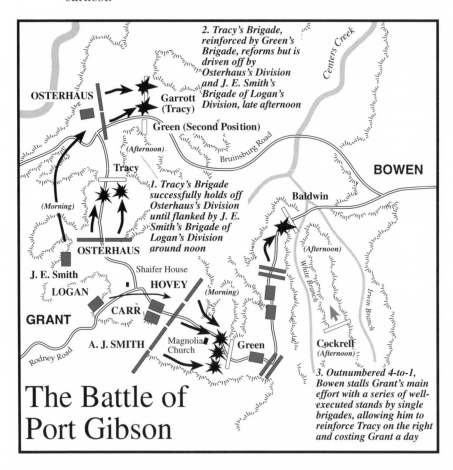

The Battle of Port Gibson

2. Tracy's Brigade, reinforced by Green's Brigade, reforms but is driven off by Osterhaus's Division and J. E. Smith's Brigade of Logan's Division, late afternoon

OSTERHAUS

Garrott (Tracy)

Green (Second Position)

(Afternoon)

Tracy

Centers Creek

Bruinsburg Road

BOWEN

1. Tracy's Brigade successfully holds off Osterhaus's Division until flanked by J. E. Smith's Brigade of Logan's Division around noon

(Morning)

OSTERHAUS

Baldwin

(Afternoon)

White Branch

Irwin Branch

J. E. Smith

LOGAN

Shaifer House

HOVEY

(Morning)

GRANT

CARR

A. J. SMITH

Magnolia Church

Green

Cockrell (Afternoon)

Rodney Road

3. Outnumbered 4-to-1, Bowen stalls Grant's main effort with a series of well-executed stands by single brigades, allowing him to reinforce Tracy on the right and costing Grant a day

Most of the Union forces moved along the Rodney Road toward Magnolia Church and the Confederate left held by Green's Brigade. Heavily outnumbered and hard-pressed in front and on both flanks, the Southerners gave way shortly after 10 o'clock. The men in butternut and gray fell back a mile and a half to where they were greeted by the welcome sight of Brigadier General William E. Baldwin's and Colonel Francis Cockrell's Brigades. Recent arrivals on the field, these rugged veterans formed a new line between White and Irwin Branches of Willow Creek. Full of fight, they reestablished the Confederate left flank and braced themselves for the Union onslaught. Green's Brigade, exhausted and badly shaken, was ordered to re-form and support the Confederate right along the Bruinsburg Road.

As morning attacks drove Green's Brigade from its position, Tracy's men watched anxiously as the Federals crept toward their position with flags flying and bayonets glistening in the sunlight. The Alabamians steadied themselves for action, and soon the fields and forest were alive as the opposing lines opened with musketry. Sergeant Francis G. Obenchain of the Botetourt (Virginia) Artillery recalled that while speaking to General Tracy, "a ball struck him on back of the neck passing through. He fell with great force on his face and in falling cried 'O Lord!' He was dead when I stooped to him." Ed Tracy thus became the first of several Confederate generals to die in the defense of Vicksburg. Colonel Isham W. Garrott assumed command of the brigade and held his men to their task.

Although Tracy was killed early in the action, his brigade, under Garrott's command, managed to hold its tenuous line throughout the morning against steadily mounting pressure. But it was clear that unless the Confederates received heavy reinforcements they would lose the day. Bowen wired his superiors: "We have been engaged in a furious battle ever since daylight; losses very heavy. The men act nobly, but the odds are overpowering."

Early afternoon found the Federal juggernaut once again in motion on the Rodney Road toward the thin gray line along Irwin Branch. Bowen's determined fighters offered stiff resistance and stalled the attack in front, but the Union lines soon extended beyond the Confederate flanks. Bowen knew that it was only a matter of time before the blue-clad mass rolled over his troops and drove them from the field.

Fearful that the Federals might reach the Natchez Road and flank him from the south, Bowen moved Cockrell's Missourians into position to strike the extreme right of the Federal line. As Union pressure built along the Rodney Road, the Missourians unleashed a vicious counterattack that began to roll up the blue line. In the smoke and confusion of battle, Cockrell's men enjoyed initial success, but it was short-lived; the counterattack ground to a halt in the face of overwhelming numbers. Unable to hold their position, the Missourians fell back as their comrades in Baldwin's Brigade desperately clung to the position along Irwin Branch.

Over on the Bruinsburg Road Colonel Garrott's Alabamians grimly held their ground as Green's weary soldiers arrived to bolster the line. Despite reinforcement, the Confederates could not stop the relentless Federal advance, which pressed their right flank and threatened to break the line. In desperation, the Sixth Missouri raised the Rebel yell and counterattacked to relieve the pressure on Garrott's men, but the odds against the lone regiment were too great. The Confederates were easily checked and forced to withdraw—the day was lost.

At 5:30 p.m. the battle-weary Southerners began to retire from the field, falling back across Bayou Pierre toward Grand Gulf. Bowen's command had suffered 60 killed, 340 wounded, and 387 missing out of the 8,000 men engaged on May 1. In addition, 4 guns of the Botetourt (Virginia) Artillery were lost. Pemberton notified the authorities in Richmond of the day's events, advising that "Large reenforcements should be sent me from other departments. Enemy's movement threatens

Jackson, and, if successful, cuts off Vicksburg and Port Hudson from the east." The Battle of Port Gibson, which cost Grant 131 killed, 719, wounded, and 25 missing, resulted in a significant Union victory. After a day of fierce combat, the Army of the Tennessee had secured its foothold on Mississippi soil and through its bold conduct established the character of future actions. Two days after the battle the Confederates evacuated Grand Gulf, leaving the strategic landing to the Federals, who turned it into a base from which to launch the next phase of the campaign for Vicksburg.

6
ONWARD TO JACKSON

The most pressing question for Grant after his victory at Port Gibson was in which direction to turn his army. The road north led directly to Vicksburg, but his keen appreciation of geography argued against this route. After crossing the Big Black River his army would be in a narrow triangle of land—bordered by the Mississippi River on the west and the Big Black to the east—that would restrict his ability to maneuver. Besides, he expected Pemberton to concentrate his forces south of Vicksburg, which was exactly what the Confederate commander struggled to do that first week of May.

Rather than march northward on Vicksburg, Grant aimed his army in a northeasterly direction. He intended to cut the Southern Railroad of Mississippi that connected Vicksburg with Jackson, severing that vital line of communications and cutting the Confederate garrison off from supplies and reinforcements. A long march, conducted with speed and precision, would carry his men deep into the heart of Mississippi. Over a seventeen-day period, often referred to as the blitzkrieg of the Vicksburg Campaign, Grant's army would march more than 200 miles, fight five battles, and drive the Confederates into the city's defenses.

Not wishing to push the march until his army was united, Grant ordered Sherman's Corps to join him without delay. While the hard-marching veterans of the XV Corps hastened to join their comrades east of the Mississippi River, the main force rested in the vicinity of Willow Springs. Grant also launched a strong demonstration at Hankinson's Ferry to keep Pemberton's attention focused south of Vicksburg. Once Sherman's men crossed the river, Grant's rugged soldiers shouldered their rifles and resumed the march.

The Union army advanced on a broad front with McClernand's Corps on the left, closest to the Big Black River, Sherman's in the center, and McPherson's on the right. When his army reached a line between Old Auburn and Raymond, Grant planned to wheel to the north and strike the railroad between Edwards and Bolton. But Pemberton divined Grant's intention and ordered a brigade from Jackson to Raymond with instructions to strike the Federals in flank or rear as they moved toward the railroad.

The morning of May 12 found McPherson's XVII Corps on the march along the road from Utica toward Raymond. Shortly before 10 a.m. the Union skirmish line swept over a ridge and moved cautiously through open fields into the valley of Fourteenmile Creek, southwest of Raymond. Suddenly, a deadly volley ripped into their ranks from the woods that lined the almost-dry stream. Confederate artillery also opened fire, announcing the presence of Brigadier General John Gregg's Brigade.

The ever combative Gregg hoped to strike with his 3,000-man brigade, turn the Federal right flank, and capture the entire force in his front. Faulty intelligence had led him to believe that he faced only a small contingent of Union troops,

JAMES B. MCPHERSON

Born Ohio 1828; McPherson was graduated from the U.S. Military Academy in 1853, first in his class of fifty-two that included J.B. Hood, P.H. Sheridan, and J.M. Schofield; commissioned a 2d lieutenant of engineers, he taught at the academy and worked on coastal fortifications; promoted to 1st lieutenant in 1858 and captain in August 1861, he retained his staff assignment following the outbreak of the Civil War; promoted to lieutenant colonel in November 1861, he was aide-de-camp to

General Henry Halleck in Missouri; he was General U.S. Grant's chief engineer during the battles at Forts Henry and Donelson, Shiloh, and in the advance on Corinth; promoted to colonel in May 1862, he entered the volunteer organization that same month as brigadier general; he commanded the Engineer Brigade, Army of the Tennessee, until his promotion to major general of volunteers in October 1862; he commanded the Seventeenth Corps, Army of the Tennessee, during the Vicksburg Campaign and was promoted to brigadier general in the regular army in August 1863; he led his corps in the Meridian Campaign and in March 1864 succeeded General W.T. Sherman as commander of the Department and Army of the Tennessee; he led the army, one of three in Sherman's conglomerate force, during the early stages of the Atlanta Campaign, but his indecisive actions at Snake Creek Gap in May and during the Battle of Peachtree Creek in July led to missed opportunities to crush the Confederate army; during the Battle of Atlanta in July 1864, General McPherson was killed by Rebel skirmishers as he rode unescorted to the scene of the fighting. A particular favorite of both Grant and Sherman, he was a loyal and dependable subordinate; as an army commander, however, he proved unequal to the responsibility.

when in reality, McPherson's 10,000-man corps occupied the road before him. Thick clouds of smoke and dust obscured the field and neither commander could accurately assess the size of the force in his front. Regardless of the odds, Gregg's fighting blood was up and he directed his troops to advance.

Shortly after noon, Gregg's regiments advanced across the creek en echelon from right to left, slamming into the opposing ranks with a vengeance. The blue line began to waver—and broke in places—but Major General John A. Logan rode forward with "the shriek of an eagle" and turned the men back to their places. Although the Confederates enjoyed initial suc-

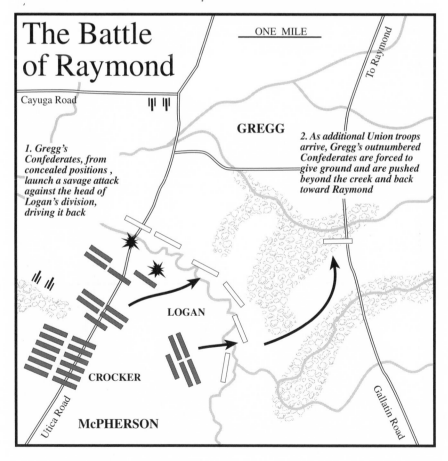

The Battle of Raymond

ONE MILE

To Raymond

Cayuga Road

GREGG

1. Gregg's Confederates, from concealed positions , launch a savage attack against the head of Logan's division, driving it back

2. As additional Union troops arrive, Gregg's outnumbered Confederates are forced to give ground and are pushed beyond the creek and back toward Raymond

LOGAN

CROCKER

Utica Road

McPHERSON

Gallatin Road

JOHN GREGG

Born Alabama 1828; attended LaGrange College, taught school, and practiced law in Tuscumbia before moving in 1854 to Texas; settled at Fairfield; married Mary Garth; elected a district judge; an ardent secessionist, he was a member of the convention that voted Texas out of the Union in 1861 and he represented the state in the provisional Congress that met in Montgomery to organize the Confederate government. After

fighting began in the summer, Gregg returned to Texas and organized the 7th Texas Infantry, which elected him its colonel; captured in 1862 along with his regiment when Fort Donelson surrendered to General Grant; after spending several months as a prisoner of war before being exchanged in August, Gregg received promotion to brigadier general and command of a brigade composed of Texas and Tennessee troops. Defended Chickasaw Bayou against Sherman's army in December; sent with his brigade to Port Hudson, La., but in May 1863 moved to join Confederate forces east of Vicksburg; Gregg's brigade engaged in the action at Jackson before being transferred to the Army of Tennessee; participated in the Battle of Chickamauga, where he was seriously wounded; when able to return to duty in 1864, he was given command of the Texas Brigade, formerly Hood's Brigade, Army of Northern Virginia. After the Battle of the Wilderness, Gregg and his men fought courageously at Spotsylvania, the North Anna River, Cold Harbor, and in defense of Petersburg; in October 1864 in an attempt to recapture part of the Confederate trenches east of Richmond, Gregg died leading an unsuccessful attack down the Darbytown Road. Brave, capable, and esteemed, Gregg was what one officer called "a born soldier."

cess, Union resistance stiffened and it became clear that a much larger Federal force was on the field. By early afternoon, the Confederate attack ground to a halt. Union forces now counterattacked.

Federal brigades continued to arrive on the field and deployed in line of battle on either side of the Utica road. In piecemeal fashion, McPherson's men pushed forward at 1:30 p.m., driving the Confederates back across Fourteenmile Creek. The fighting that ensued was of the most confused nature. Due to the dense vegetation that lined the stream and the thick smoke of battle, neither commander knew where their units were or what they were doing. Ultimately, Union numerical superiority prevailed. Under tremendous pressure, the Confederate right flank along the Utica road broke and Gregg had no alternative but to retire from the field.

The fight at Raymond cost Gregg 73 killed, 252 wounded, and 190 missing, most of whom were from the 3d Tennessee and 7th Texas. As his regiments retreated through the tree-shaded streets of town with the enemy in pursuit, Gregg's soldiers were unable to partake of the feast prepared for them by the citizens of Raymond in anticipation of their victory. Rather, much to the townspeople's chagrin, hungry Ohio soldiers enjoyed the picnic as their "victors" fled out the Jackson road to the northeast. Exhausted by the day's events, the weary Confederates fell to the ground and bivouacked for the night near Snake Creek. The following day, Gregg's brigade tramped into Jackson.

There was no Federal pursuit past Raymond; McPherson's troops bedded down for the night in and around the town. In this, his first fight as a corps commander, McPherson lost 446 men of whom 68 were killed, 341 wounded, and 37 missing. Content with the day's results, the XVII Corps' commander had his men bury the dead and remove the wounded from the field.

The engagement at Raymond led Grant to change the direction of his army's march. He now decided to move on Jackson, intending to destroy the Mississippi capital's rail communications and scatter any Confederate reinforcements who might be on the way to Vicksburg. McPherson's Corps moved north through Raymond to Clinton on May 13, while Sherman pushed northeast through Raymond to Mississippi Springs. To cover the march on Jackson, Grant placed McClernand's Corps in a defensive posture, facing west on a line from Raymond through Bolton to Clinton.

Late in the afternoon of May 13, as the Federals closed on Jackson, a train carrying Confederate General Joseph E. Johnston arrived in the capital (In response to the Federal threat, Governor John J. Pettus had moved the seat of state government to Enterprise). Ordered to Mississippi by

JOHN A. LOGAN

Born Illinois 1826; Logan studied law and served as a volunteer officer during the Mexican War; he entered the Illinois legislature and in 1858 was elected to the U.S. House of Representatives; a Democrat, he whole-heartedly supported the Union; during the First Battle of Bull Run, while still a civilian, he picked up a musket and joined the fighting; he then raised a regiment that became the 31st Illinois and he became its colonel; he fought at Belmont and was wounded at Fort Donelson; promoted to brigadier general, U.S. Volunteers, in March 1862, he resigned his congressional seat and returned to action during the operations at Corinth, Mississippi; promoted to major general of volunteers in November 1862, he commanded a division in the Army of the Tennessee during the Vicksburg Campaign; he commanded the Fifteenth Corps, Army of the Tennessee, during the Atlanta Campaign of 1864; when General J.B. McPherson was killed during the Battle of Atlanta, Logan assumed command of the army, rallying the shattered force to victory;

President Davis, Johnston was to salvage the rapidly deteriorating situation. He established his headquarters in the Bowman House, where he was apprised of available troop strengths and the condition of the fortifications around Jackson. Johnston immediately wired the Richmond authorities, "I am too late." Instead of fighting for Jackson, he ordered the city evacuated. Gregg was to fight a delaying action to cover the evacuation.

A heavy rain fell during the night, turning the roads into ribbons of mud. Advancing slowly under cloudy skies, Sherman's and McPherson's Corps converged on Jackson by mid-morning of May 14. Around 9 o'clock the lead elements of McPherson's Corps were fired upon by Confederate artillery

despite his performance and his acknowledged ability on the battlefield, General W.T. Sherman passed over Logan, who was not a West Pointer, for permanent command of the Army of the Tennessee, opting instead for General O.O. Howard; although embittered, Logan returned to his corps and led it with great skill for the remainder of the campaign; after the fall of Atlanta, he took a leave to campaign for President Abraham Lincoln's reelection; he rejoined his command at Savannah and led the Fifteenth Corps throughout the Carolinas Campaign of 1865; after leading the Army of the Tennessee in the Grand Review at Washington, he resigned his volunteer commission in August 1865; declining a brigadier generalcy in the regular army, he returned to politics as a Republican; he served in both the House and Senate and was an unsuccessful vice presidential candidate in 1884; dedicated to veteran's affairs, he was prominent in the Grand Army of the Republic; he also wrote extensively on the war, including *The Volunteer Soldier of America* that extolled the virtues of the volunteer over the professional soldier; General Logan died at Washington in 1886. Clearly one of the most effective of the so-called "political generals," Logan was an outstanding combat commander; his lack of a West Point pedigree no doubt cost him an army command.

posted on the O.P. Wright farm, northwest of the city. A flurry of activity ensued as McPherson prepared to attack. But the rain continued to fall in sheets, threatening to spoil his soldiers' ammunition by soaking the powder in their paper-wrapped cartridges. Reluctantly, he postponed the attack until the rain stopped.

As the downpour ceased around 11:00 a.m., bugles sounded the advance. Raising a mighty cheer, the Federals sprang forward with bayonets fixed and banners unfurled. In a bitter

JOSEPH E. JOHNSTON

Born Virginia 1807; Johnston was graduated from the U.S. Military Academy in 1829, thirteenth in his class of forty-six; commissioned a 2d lieutenant of artillery, he served on the frontier and against the Seminoles in Florida; he left the service in 1837 to become a civil engineer but returned the following year as 1st lieutenant of topographical engineers; promoted to captain in 1846, he fought with conspicuous bravery during the Mexican War, suffering five wounds and receiving three brevets for gallantry; after years of service on the frontier, in 1855 he became lieutenant colonel of 1st Cavalry; in 1860 he was appointed quartermaster general with the staff rank of brigadier general (his substantive rank remained lieutenant colonel) but in April 1861, with the secession of Virginia, he resigned to serve his native state; appointed a major general in the Virginia state forces, Johnston entered Confederate service as a brigadier general in May 1861 and took command of the Harpers Ferry garrison; he led this force to Manassas Junction, where he became senior officer during the first major battle of the war; promoted to full general in July 1861, he was upset to find he ranked fourth among the Confederacy's generals (he believed that his staff rank in the U.S. Army dictated that he be first in seniority); this triggered a conflict with President Jefferson Davis that would last the rest of their lives; this notwithstanding, Johnston led the primary Rebel

hand-to-hand struggle, McPherson's men overwhelmed Gregg's Southerners and forced them back into the Jackson fortifications. After a brief pause to reform, the Northern soldiers cautiously approached the city's defenses only to find that they had been abandoned.

Sherman's Corps meanwhile reached Lynch Creek, southwest of Jackson, at 11 o'clock, when the shrill whistle of artillery shells announced the presence of Confederate troops in the open fields north of the stream. Union cannon were

army during the Peninsular Campaign of 1862 and had retreated to the outskirts of Richmond before he was wounded in the Battle of Seven Pines; General Robert E. Lee assumed command and fought a bloody campaign to save the capital; returning to duty, Johnston was ordered to take command of the Department of the West, a huge command that included all Confederate forces between the Appalachian Mountains and the Mississippi; he failed to mount a serious effort to relieve Federal pressure on Vicksburg in the summer of 1863; after the disaster at Missionary Ridge he replaced General Braxton Bragg as commander of the Army of Tennessee; during the early stages of the 1864 Atlanta Campaign, Johnston conducted a skillful strategic withdrawal that frustrated Davis, who wanted an offensive; after retreating to the vicinity of Atlanta, Johnston was relieved and replaced by General John B. Hood; recalled to duty by Lee in early 1865, Johnston opposed General W.T. Sherman in North Carolina before surrendering in April; following the war he engaged in numerous business activities, served in the U.S. House of Representatives from Virginia (1879-1881), and was a U.S. railroad commissioner (1885-1891); he devoted much of his time to defending his actions during the war and attacking Davis and Hood; to this end he published several articles and an extensive memoir, *Narrative of Military Operations* (1874); he died at Washington in 1891 of complications from a cold he reportedly contracted while attending Sherman's funeral. Immensely popular, Johnston enjoyed a splendid reputation, largely the result of his own writings; he was a gifted organizer and a master of the strategic withdrawal; but, while personally brave in the extreme, he was reluctant to risk offensive action.

rushed forward and in short order compelled the Confederates to seek shelter behind the city's defenses. But, failing to destroy a narrow wooden bridge across the bank-full stream, the Southern soldiers provided Sherman's men with the means to cross Lynch Creek.

Once across the creek, the Federals reformed their lines and advanced slowly at 2:00 p.m., but soon were stopped by canister fire. Not wishing to expose his men to such deadly fire, Sherman sent one regiment to the right (east) in search of a weak spot in the enemy line. The men of the 95th Ohio moved off through the woods until they reached the tracks of the New Orleans, Jackson & Great Northern Railroad, then turned and nervously approached the Confederate fortifications. As they scaled the parapet, the Ohioans were greatly relieved to find the works deserted.

An elderly black man greeted Federal troops with the news that the Rebels had departed and the city was their's for the taking. In disbelief, one Ohioan asked, "Why are the Rebs still firing their battery if they had left the place?" Laughing in response, the man replied, "Oh! There is only a few cannoneers there to work the guns to keep you back." True enough, the Federals discovered only a handful of state troops and civilian volunteers at the guns and took them prisoner, clearing the way for their comrades to enter Jackson.

The Confederates were well out the Canton Road to the north when Union troops entered Jackson around 3 o'clock. McPherson's men unfurled the Stars and Stripes atop the capitol to symbolize their victory. In the short, but spirited, engagement at Jackson, Federal casualties totaled 300 men, of whom 42 were killed, 251 wounded, and 7 missing. Confederate casualties were not accurately reported, but were estimated at 845 killed, wounded and missing. In addition, 17 pieces of artillery fell into Union hands.

To avoid the use of experienced combat troops on occupation duty, Grant ordered Jackson neutralized militarily. The torch was applied to machine shops and factories, telegraph lines were cut, and railroad tracks destroyed. All facilities that supported the war effort were burned, including a textile factory in which women rolled out cloth marked "C.S.A." Grant, who was visiting the facility with Sherman, turned to his trusted corps commander and suggested that the women had done enough work. Prior to burning the factory, the generals permitted the women to leave and take with them all the cloth they could carry. Entrusting the destruction to Sherman's Corps, Grant now turned his other two corps west toward his primary objective—Vicksburg.

7
DISASTER AND DISGRACE

During the two weeks that followed the Federal landing at Bruinsburg, Confederate Commander John Pemberton endeavored to concentrate his forces for the defense of Vicksburg and stockpile supplies in the city. He had yielded the initiative to a dangerous opponent, whose forces had pushed deep into the interior of Mississippi, overwhelmed the resistance at Port Gibson and Raymond, and had captured the capital city of Jackson. Now Pemberton intended to meet Grant east of Vicksburg along the line of the Big Black River. With his troops dug in on the high ground west of the river, he hoped to check Grant's attack, then counterattack and drive the Union army into the interior of the state, where, away from its supplies and without the protection of the fleet, it could be destroyed.

Pemberton, though, was a Northerner by birth and was well aware of the distrust of him that existed among his subordinates. Indecisive by nature, he allowed this knowledge to con-

trol him. He called councils of war to determine what course
of action his officers would support. His division commanders
were eager to move against the invaders and recommended an
advance beyond the Big Black River. Spurred by his more
aggressive subordinates, Pemberton ordered the advance
against his better judgement.

On May 12, the day of the Battle of Raymond, Pemberton
issued a circular to the army in which he announced "The hour
of trial has come!" Appealing to his soldier's sense of duty,
honor, and love of family, the commanding general sought to
inspire his men to feats of courage in the coming fray. In closing, he assured his troops: "Soldiers! be vigilant, brave and
active; let there be no cowards, nor laggards, nor stragglers
from the ranks—and the God of battle will certainly crown our
efforts with success." Fueled by such an appeal, his men
shouldered their muskets and took up the line of march across
the Big Black River to Edwards Station. Leaving a sizeable
force behind to defend Vicksburg, Pemberton took the field
with only three of his five divisions—hardly a match for Grant's
Army of the Tennessee.

Early on the morning of May 16, 1863, General Grant
received news that Confederate forces were at Edwards
Station and prepared to march east. He ordered his columns
forward to converge on Edwards. Moving westward from
Bolton and Raymond, Federal soldiers pushed in three parallel
columns over roads that had dried since the May 14 cloud-
burst. About 7 a.m. the southernmost column made contact
with Confederate pickets near the Davis plantation on the
Raymond-Edwards Road and shots rang out. The Battle of
Champion Hill, the largest, bloodiest, and most significant
action of the Vicksburg campaign had opened.

The sounds of battle intensified as the opposing forces also
made contact on the Middle Road. Pemberton was forced to
stand his ground. He deployed his divisions along a three-mile
front on a line running southwest to northeast that guarded

both the Raymond-Edwards and Middle roads and commanded the valley of Jackson Creek. If the Federals advanced along these two roads alone, Pemberton's position would be tough to break. Unfortunately for the Pennsylvania-born Confederate, another powerful Union column was pushing along the Jackson Road toward his left flank, undetected.

Shortly after 9 a.m. a courier brought news of the Federal advance along the Jackson Road. In response, Pemberton shifted troops to the left to cover Champion Hill. As the Confederates moved into position on the bald crest of the hill, Federal soldiers reached the Champion house and swung from

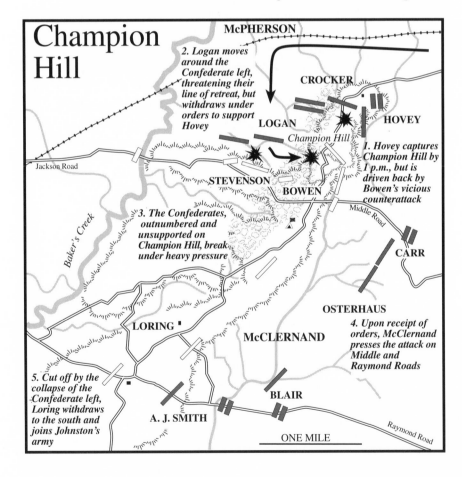

Champion Hill

McPHERSON

2. Logan moves around the Confederate left, threatening their line of retreat, but withdraws under orders to support Hovey

CROCKER

LOGAN

HOVEY

Champion Hill

Jackson Road

1. Hovey captures Champion Hill by 1 p.m., but is driven back by Bowen's vicious counterattack

STEVENSON

BOWEN

Baker's Creek

Middle Road

3. The Confederates, outnumbered and unsupported on Champion Hill, break under heavy pressure

CARR

OSTERHAUS

LORING

McCLERNAND

4. Upon receipt of orders, McClernand presses the attack on Middle and Raymond Roads

5. Cut off by the collapse of the Confederate left, Loring withdraws to the south and joins Johnston's army

A. J. SMITH

BLAIR

ONE MILE

Raymond Road

column into double line of battle. Seeing that the Southerners held the commanding hill in their front, Union artillerymen quickly wheeled their guns into position and unlimbered. The bloodshed began in earnest as these batteries came to life.

Grant arrived near the Champion house around 10 o'clock, and after surveying the situation, he ordered the attack. Two Union divisions in battle array, 10,000 men strong, moved forward in magnificent style with flags flying. The long blue lines extended westward beyond the Confederate flank and posed a grave threat to the troops on Champion Hill. To meet this danger, Confederate Brigadier General Stephen D. Lee shifted his Alabamians farther to the west, creating a gap between his brigade and the troops who defended the vital crossroads south of Champion Hill.

By 11:30 the Northerners reached the base of Champion Hill and closed on the Confederate line. With a mighty cheer the Federals stormed the position and with bayonets glistening in the sunlight charged among the Southerners. The lines swayed back and forth as charge met countercharge. But the strength of numbers prevailed, and the blue tide swept over the crest of Champion Hill shortly after 1 p.m.

The Confederates fell back in disorder to the Jackson Road, followed by the hard-driving Federals. The powerful Union drive captured the Crossroads and, on the right, severed the Jackson Road escape route over rain-swollen Bakers Creek. Confronted by disaster, Pemberton ordered his two remaining divisions to counterattack. Leaving one brigade to guard the Raymond Road, the Confederates moved from their right along the Ratliff Road toward the Crossroads.

Stifling clouds of dust choked the 4,500 soldiers of Bowen's Division as they rushed past army headquarters, where a small group of women sang "Dixie" to inspire the troops. With characteristic abandon, Colonel Cockrell, carrying a large magnolia blossom in one hand, led the way. His men hit the Federals near the Crossroads. At the point of bayonet they drove their enemy back three-quarters of a mile and regained control of Champion Hill. But the attack was made with insufficient numbers and it faltered short of the Champion house.

To contain the breakthrough, Grant ordered up fresh troops. In addition, the Federals along Middle and Raymond Roads began to advance in force. All morning, these troops had acted under instructions to "move cautiously," but were now thrown forward, advancing in overwhelming numbers on both roads. In a matter of moments Confederate resistance was shattered and Pemberton ordered his army from the field.

With only one avenue of escape open to them, the Confederates fled toward the Raymond Road crossing of Bakers Creek. Brigadier General Lloyd Tilghman's Brigade, acting as the rear guard for the army, was ordered to hold its ground at all costs. In so doing, Tilghman was killed and his brigade, along with the rest of Loring's Division, was cut off from Edwards. Desperate to escape, these men turned south on a plantation road, marched through the night, and eventually made their way to Jackson by a circuitous route.

The victorious Federals gained control of the Bakers Creek bridge late in the afternoon and pushed on in pursuit of the retreating Confederates. About 8 p.m. Union soldiers entered Edwards, which was illuminated by the blaze from commissary supplies and quartermaster stores set afire by Pemberton's forces. With the town secured, the soldiers bedded down for the night for some much needed rest, their dreams sweetened by the victory they had won. But their success at Champion Hill had cost them 410 killed, 1,844 wounded, and 187 missing out of 32,000 men.

May 16 proved a disastrous day for Pemberton. His army lost 381 men killed, 1,018 wounded, and 2,441 missing out of the 25,000 men engaged. In addition, 27 pieces of artillery were lost. Equally important, Pemberton lost his poise and was badly shaken by the defeat at Champion Hill; he sought now only to run for the protection of the Vicksburg defenses.

Full of despair, he rode west through the darkness. Perhaps he realized, as British General J.F.C. Fuller observed a century later, that "The drums of Champion's [sic] Hill sounded the doom of Richmond."

LLOYD TILGHMAN

Born Maryland 1816; Tilghman was graduated from the U.S. Military Academy in 1836, forty-sixth in his class of forty-nine; posted to the 1st Dragoons, the resigned his 2d lieutenant's commission only weeks later to become a railroad engineer; during the War with Mexico, he served on the staff of General David Twiggs and as a captain in the Maryland and District of Columbia Battalion; following the war he returned to railroad engineering, mostly in Panama; in 1852 he settled in Kentucky, where he was active in the state's military organization; following the outbreak of the Civil War, Tilghman offered his services to the Confederacy and was appointed brigadier general in October 1861; assigned to Kentucky, he grew concerned over the tenuous nature of Confederate defenses on the Tennessee and Cumberland Rivers; charged with improving the works at Forts Henry and Donelson, he found his authority encumbered  and the process frustrating; when Union Flag Officer Andrew Foote's gun-boats approached Fort Henry in February 1862, Tilghman sent most of the garrison to Fort Donelson, and with some 100 men put up a spirited defense, often serving the guns himself, before surrendering; not exchanged until August 1862, he commanded rendezvous and instruction camps before heading a brigade at Corinth and in the retreat from Holly Springs; during the Vicksburg Campaign, he commanded a brigade in General W.W. Loring's Division; in the fighting at Champion Hill, again per-sonally working a cannon, Tilghman was killed when a Federal shell frag-ment tore through his body; a magnificent equestrian statue on the grounds of Vicksburg National Military Park commemorates the general's last stand.

Late that night, John A. Leavy, a Confederate surgeon, took pen in hand to write in the pages of his diary critical observations of Pemberton and the Battle of Champion Hill. "Today proved to the nation the value of a general," he began, "Pemberton is either a traitor, or the most incompetent officer in the confederacy. *Indecision, Indedecision* (sic), *Indecision.*" He lamented that, "We have been badly defeated where we might have given the enemy a severe repulse. We have been defeated in detail, and have lost, O God! how many brave and gallant soldiers." Leavy's sentiments were echoed by hundreds of soldiers who streamed toward the fortress city on the river, cursing their commanding general: "It's all Pem's fault."

Throughout the night, Confederate soldiers staggered toward the Big Black River en route to Vicksburg. East of the stream, on low, flat ground, a strong line of fortifications had been constructed earlier in the year to protect the railroad bridge against possible attack by Grierson's raiders. Pemberton ordered Bowen's Division and a fresh brigade commanded by Brigadier General John Vaughn to man the fortifications and hold the bridges long enough for Loring's men to cross. Unbeknownst to Pemberton, Loring was not marching toward the river. Instead, Federal troops appeared early in the morning and prepared to storm the defenses.

At an early hour on May 17 reveille sounded throughout the Federal camps around Edwards and soon the troops were on the road in hot pursuit of the Confederates. McClernand's XIII Corps led the march and, as the men neared Big Black River, they spotted the enemy posted behind earthworks. Bristling with bayonets, the line appeared formidable. McClernand quickly deployed his units astride the road and artillery opened on the Confederate fortifications with solid shot and shell.

Federal Brigadier General Michael Lawler moved his brigade into position on the Union right and deployed his soldiers in a meander scar near the river. The depression that sheltered his men was only a few yards in front of the

Confederate works. Ordering his troops to fix bayonets, Lawler bellowed, "Forward!" Like lightning, his men sprang out of the depression and, in a matter of minutes, advanced across the field, filtered through the obstruction of trees that fronted the works, and swarmed over the Confederate fortifications.

Startled by the assault, the Southerners broke and ran to the rear. Throwing aside their weapons and accouterments, they fled toward the bridges; many jumped into the river only to be swallowed by the turbid water. The Southern army lost almost 1,800 men as prisoners, 18 cannon, six limbers, four caissons, and five battle flags at Big Black River. The Federals suffered less than 300 casualties. Fortunately for the Confederates, Major Samuel Lockett, the army's chief engineer, set fire to the railroad bridge and the steamer *Dot*, moored across the river as an improvised boat bridge, in time to check pursuing Union troops. With the bridges in flames, Pemberton and what was left of his field army fell back to Vicksburg.

Overwhelmed by despair, the Confederate commander rode silently from the field of battle. Having witnessed the debacle at the Big Black River and the wild flight of his troops, Pemberton remarked to a member of his staff, "Just thirty years ago I began my military career by receiving my appointment to a cadetship at the U.S. Military Academy, and to-day— that same date—that career is ended in disaster and disgrace." For all practical purposes it was, but it was a disaster that would affect an entire nation.

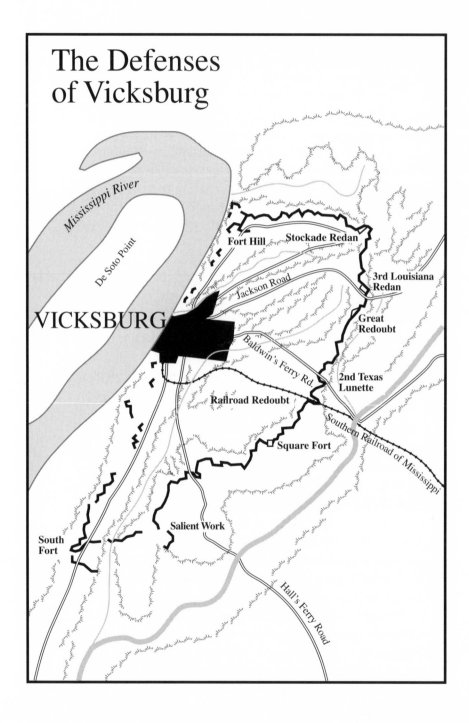

The Defenses of Vicksburg

8
FORTRESS VICKSBURG
STANDS DEFIANT

The citizens of Vicksburg watched in fear as the shattered remnants of Pemberton's army poured into the city on May 17. Mrs. Emma Balfour, wife of a prominent Vicksburg physician, stood in her doorway on that fateful day as the demoralized mass of humanity filled the streets. She later wrote, "I hope never to witness again such a scene as the return of our routed army!" She recorded the scene that enveloped her, "From twelve o'clock until late in the night the streets and roads were *jammed* with wagons, cannons, horses, men, mules, stock, sheep, everything you can imagine that appertains to an army being brought hurriedly within the intrenchment," adding, "Nothing like order prevailed, of course, as divisions, brigades and regiments were broken and separated."

The shocked citizenry of Vicksburg slowly pieced together

the details of the battles at Champion Hill and Big Black River Bridge. To those who listened to the woeful details, one fact became apparent. The incisive Mrs. Balfour, sensitive of the discontentment with General Pemberton then freely expressed by soldiers and officers alike, recorded the essence of failure: "I knew from all I saw and heard that it was want of confidence in the General commanding that was the cause of our disaster." Late that night, overcome with emotion, she confided to her diary the fears of many in Vicksburg. "What is to become of all the living things in this place...shut up as in a trap," she wrote, "God only knows."

Through the long day and into the evening marched Pemberton's weary soldiers. Singly or in small groups, with no sense of order or discipline, the men filed into the rifle pits and turned to meet Grant's rapidly approaching army. A medley of sounds filled the night air as the Confederates readied their defenses: officers shouted orders, teamsters whipped their animals and dragged artillery into position, and, as the soldiers worked with picks and shovels, some men cursed while others prayed. Throughout the night, the ringing of axes was constant as additional trees were felled to strengthen fortifications, clear fields of fire, and form abatis* in their front. Work continued at a feverish pace and by sunrise the city was in a good state of defense.

Late in the afternoon on May 18, Confederate soldiers spotted long columns of Union infantry moving slowly toward the city. It was a terrifying spectacle, and yet somehow beautiful,

---

* Abatis was a dense obstruction of felled trees toppled toward likely avenues of enemy approach. The branches were stripped and sharpened and an entanglement of telegraph wire was strung among or in front of the limbs. The purpose of the abatis was to disrupt approaching lines of infantry. At best, the Federal soldiers would be able to filter their way through the obstruction singly or in small groups. Once on the other side of the abatis, now in the clear field of fire, they would be easy targets for Confederate infantrymen posted behind stout fortifications. The abatis would have the desired effect.

as battle flags snapped in the breeze above the columns and bayonets glistened in the sunlight. Union skirmishers quickly deployed and artillery roared into action; but the day wore away with nothing more than a long range artillery duel. That night, as darkness enveloped the fields, the soldiers of both armies rested on their arms. Each knew that the bloody work at hand would commence with the rising sun and each prepared for battle in his own way.

William Lovelace Foster, a chaplain in the 35th Mississippi Infantry, captured the varied emotions of the evening in the leaves of his journal:

> That night was a solemn night for the soldier. None but those who have had the experience can tell the feeling of the soldier's heart on the night before the approaching battle—when upon the wings of fond imagination his soul visits the loved ones at home—and while he thinks of a lonely & loving wife whose face he may never look upon again & who may never see his form any more on earth, his heart bleeds & dark forebodings fill his mind. Then when he lies down upon the cold ground & looks up to the shining stars above, the gloomy thought crosses his mind, that it may be the last time he will ever look upon the shining heavens & that those same stars which now look down so quiet upon him, may behold him on the morrow night a lifeless, mangled corpse. If he be a child of God, he will commit his soul to God & implore his protection. If a wicked man he will review the past with remorse & the future with dread & will form a weak resolution to do better from that day if God will spare his life through the battle.

FRANCIS P. BLAIR, JR.

Born Kentucky 1821; graduated from Princeton in 1841, Frank Blair studied law at Transylvania University in Kentucky and opened a practice in St.Louis; he staunchly opposed secession and the expansion of slavery into the territories and actively worked against both; he served two terms in the U.S. House of Representatives and was a strong supporter of Abraham Lincoln; his brother Montgomery was Lincoln's first postmaster general; he led Missouri's pro-Union faction and with Nathaniel Lyon directed the seizure of the St.Louis arsenal and pro-secession forces at Camp Jackson; largely at his own expense he raised seven regiments for Federal service and in August 1862 was appointed brigadier general of U.S. Volunteers; promoted to major general in November, he commanded a brigade and then a division during the Vicksburg Campaign; during the Chattanooga Campaign he headed the Fifteenth Corps, Army of the Tennessee; as commander of the Seventeenth Corps, he performed with marked distinction during the Atlanta Campaign of 1864, and played a major role in the July Battle of Atlanta; he continued to direct the Seventeenth Corps during General W.T. Sherman's March to the Sea and in the Carolinas Campaign of 1865; he resigned his volunteer commission in November 1865; at war's end Blair was financially ruined, having spent his personal fortune in support of the Union; he also fell into disfavor with radical Republicans for his opposition to heavy-handed reconstruction policies; Blair, who favored more lenient readmission terms for Confederate states, was twice nominated for governmental posts by President Andrew Johnson but failed to win confirmation from the vindictive Senate; finally in 1871 he was selected to fill an unexpired term in the U.S. Senate but long plagued by poor heath he resigned in 1873 and died at St. Louis in 1875; he was one of several civilian or "political" generals to render excellent service during the Civil War.

Grant was anxious for a quick victory and, after making a hasty reconnaissance, he ordered an attack. But only one of his three corps, Sherman's, was in proper position to make the attack. The XV Corps would advance virtually unsupported. In preparation for the charge, Union artillery opened fire upon the city early on the morning of May 19, and for hours bombarded the Confederate works with solid shot and shell. Thick smoke from the guns shrouded the fields, making it virtually impossible to see. While the artillery hammered away at the enemy's defenses, Union infantrymen steadied their nerves and prepared to face death.

At 2:00 p.m. the guns fell silent and Union soldiers deployed into line of battle astride Graveyard Road, northeast of Vicksburg. With steady cadence, the determined soldiers of now Major General Frank Blair's Division led the advance as Sherman's Corps stormed toward the city's defenses. Pushing through a cornfield north of the road were the men of the 1st Battalion, 13th United States Infantry, one of only two Regular Army units then with Grant at Vicksburg. Led by their gallant captain, Edward Washington, the Regulars followed their colors into a deep ravine that fronted the Confederate fortifications, worked their way through the obstruction of felled trees, and clawed their way up the slope toward Stockade Redan. Braving a murderous fire, a handful of the Regulars reached the ditch in front of the fort and planted their colors on the exterior slope, the first Northern unit to do so. (Following the siege, the men of the 1st Battalion, 13th U.S. Infantry were ordered to inscribe on their flag the honor "First at Vicksburg." So proud were the officers and men of this distinction, that they adopted it as their unit motto. To this date, "First at Vicksburg" is emblazoned on the shoulder patches of the men of the 13th U.S. Infantry.)

Once in the ditch, the Federals began to dig holes in the slope with their bayonets for the purpose of scaling the bastion's exterior, but they waited for additional troops to arrive before daring such an effort. A few men from the 83d Indiana and 127th Illinois also reached the ditch and planted their colors. Still, the number of troops in the ditch was insufficient to attempt a scaling of Stockade Redan's earthen walls. The majority of Blair's Division was pinned to the ground less than 100 yards from the Confederate works and, at such close range, the lethal exchange of fire continued throughout the afternoon.

The hot afternoon sun beat unmercifully upon the troops pinned along Graveyard Road. Sweat streamed down the blackened faces of the men, many of whom had torn their last cartridge, and the desperate cry for ammunition was heard above the din of battle. In the 55th Illinois, a young musician named Orion P. Howe was one of four men who volunteered to run to the rear and call up a fresh supply of cartridges. Three of the

ORION P. HOWE

Orion P. Howe. *(pictured with Colonel Oscar Malmborg, 55th Illinois.)* During the intense fighting on May 19, 1863, fourteen-year-old drummer Orion Howe of Company C, 55th Illinois Infantry, and three others volunteered to run to the rear for badly needed ammunition. Howe was severely wounded and his three companions were killed, but the boy managed to attract the attention of General William T. Sherman, who ordered the requested cartridges rushed to the front. Sherman was moved by Howe's bravery and cited his efforts in reports to Secretary of War Edwin Stanton. After recovering, Howe served briefly on General Giles Smith's staff and later received, at Sherman's suggestion, an appointment to the U.S. Naval Academy. In 1896 Howe was awarded the Medal of Honor for his actions thirty-three years before at Vicksburg.

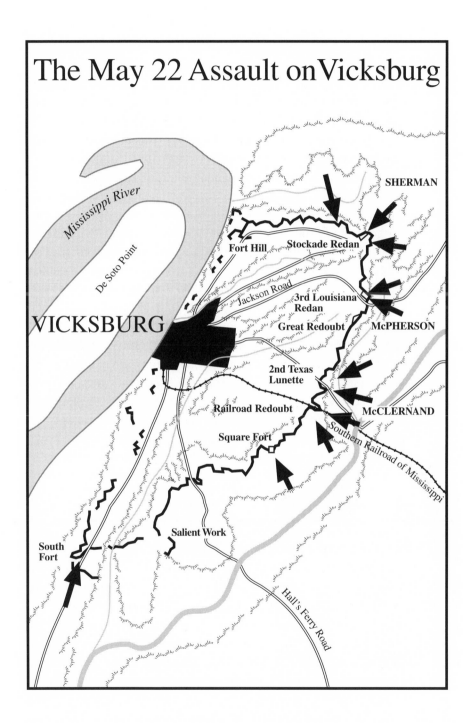

The May 22 Assault on Vicksburg

men were killed outright; but Howe, though wounded, managed to reach the rear and report the desperate situation. Heavy crates of ammunition were run forward and precious cartridges were distributed to the men on the firing line—all to no avail. Sherman's troops were repulsed with the loss of 942 men.

Undaunted by the failure to capture Vicksburg on May 19, Grant made a more thorough reconnaissance and three days later hurled his entire force against the city's defenses. Early on the morning of May 22 Federal artillery opened fire and for four hours pounded the works with solid shot and shell, tearing large holes in the earthen fortifications. As the thick smoke of the guns obscured the field, Union corps commanders readied their men for the assault. Sherman's troops once again steadied themselves to storm the Stockade Redan; McPherson's Corps formed a dense column along and south of the Jackson Road and prepared to strike both the Third Louisiana Redan and Great Redoubt that guarded the main thoroughfare into Vicksburg (the Great Redoubt was the largest, most formidable work in the Vicksburg defenses). McClernand's men focused their attention on the Second Texas Lunette and the Railroad Redoubt that covered Baldwin Ferry Road and overlooked the Southern Railroad of Mississippi respectively.

At 10 a.m., the prearranged time for the assault to begin, the artillery fell silent. Union soldiers raised a mighty cheer and moved forward over a three-mile front toward the Vicksburg defenses. Preceding Sherman's main force down Graveyard Road were 150 volunteers carrying bundles of cane, planks, and ladders with which to bridge the ditch that fronted Stockade Redan and enable the infantry to scale the bastion's walls. Dubbed the "forlorn hope," the volunteers raced along the road with their rifles slung over their shoulders. Scores of men were killed or wounded, but those who went unhurt jumped into the ditch and threw the scaling ladders against the walls. Only a handful of the supporting troops reached the ditch and, although they succeeded in planting one stand of

OLD ABE

Old Abe. *(pictured with members of the 8th Wisconsin Infantry.)* Presented to Company C of the 8th Wisconsin Infantry, this young American eagle was named in honor of President Abraham Lincoln and became the regimental mascot. Old Abe accompanied the regiment on the march and into battle, carried on a perch next to the colors. During a fight, the war eagle reportedly flew above, screaming at the enemy. He saw action at Iuka, Corinth, and throughout the Vicksburg Campaign. "Mustered out" in the fall of 1864, the eagle was presented to the governor of Wisconsin and took up residence in the state capitol. In 1881 Old Abe inhaled noxious fumes during a fire in the capitol and died a few months later. Stuffed and placed under glass, he went back on display until another fire, in 1904, destroyed his remains. Old Abe is immortalized on the shoulder patch of the 101st Airborne Division—the "Screaming Eagles." Of the many markers to honor the war eagle, the most impressive is the six-foot-tall likeness atop the Wisconsin monument at Vicksburg National Military Park.

colors on the exterior slopes of Stockade Redan, the attack
was contained easily—stopped well short of the objective.

McPherson's troops met a similar fate along the Jackson
Road. Charging down the road in a tightly packed column, four
men abreast, the soldiers of the XVII Corps braved a murderous fire of musketry. Despite their determined effort they were
driven back with heavy loss, having never reached the Third
Louisiana Redan.

South of the Jackson Road, Federal Brigadier General John
D. Stevenson's Brigade was able to deploy in a sheltered
ravine only 200 yards from Great Redoubt. Under a scorching
sun, the rugged infantrymen raised a shout and surged up the
steep hill with scaling ladders in hand. The 7th Missouri (U.S.)
Infantry, led by Captain Robert Buchanan, advanced beneath a
green flag emblazoned with a golden harp, symbolic of the
men's Irish heritage. Although casualties were high, especially
among officers in the brigade, the soldiers leaped into the
ditch and planted their colors on the exterior slope. But the
advance came to an abrupt halt as the men discovered that the
ladders were too short for the job. Those who could climbed
out of the ditch and streamed to the rear; others clung to their
precarious position and suffered through hours of "living hell"
until cover of darkness enabled them to run to safety.

On McClernand's front, farther south along the lines, the
Federals managed to reach the enemy works in force. Shouting
"Vicksburg or hell," scores of men reached the ditch before the
2d Texas Lunette, and there a furious battle raged as soldiers
of both armies fought to prevail. Corporal Thomas Higgins carried the colors of the 99th Illinois forward and planted them
atop the parapet south of the lunette, where both he and his
banner were captured. In the maelstrom of battle, artillerists
of the Chicago Mercantile Battery performed an incredible feat
as they hauled a brass 6-pounder to within 30 feet of the
lunette and fired canister at the Confederate defenders. Despite
such heroics, the Federals were repulsed with frightful loss.

Only at Railroad Redoubt did McClernand's troops force their way into the Confederate works. Lieutenant J. M. Pearson of the 30th Alabama described the attack: "Suddenly the roar of the guns ceased....I sprang to my feet and looked in the direction of the enemy, when they seemed to be springing from the bowels of the earth a long line of indigo a magnificent line in each direction, and they kept for a while the alignment as on dress parade, but moving at the double quick." The lieutenant expressed the thoughts of many as he added, "It was a grand and appalling sight."

Waves of blue-clad soldiers swept over rugged terrain and poured into the ditch in front of Railroad Redoubt. Clawing their way up the exterior slope, Sergeants Joseph Griffith and Nicholas Messenger of the 22d Iowa led a dozen men through a breach in the wall. In a desperate hand-to-hand struggle the Iowans forced the Confederates to abandon the fort, taking Lieutenant Pearson and some of his troops prisoner.

The Federals appeared on the brink of victory, but McClernand had no reserves with which to exploit his success. The crusty corps commander scribbled a note to Grant, stating "We have part possession of two forts, and the Stars and Stripes are floating over them." He implored that "A vigorous push ought to be made all along the line." Although he doubted the veracity of McClernand's information, Grant nonetheless ordered the assaults renewed.

Early in the afternoon, Federal soldiers again advanced all along the line but with no more success than they had experienced that morning. The only result of their effort was a lengthened casualties list. The fighting slowly ebbed as the sun set in the western sky and by nightfall the sounds of battle were replaced by the cries of the wounded who littered the field. In the assault on May 22, Grant lost 3,199 men killed, wounded, or missing. Confederate casualties could not have exceeded 500.

Although his army had been dealt a severe blow, Grant was

not yet willing to back down and settle for a siege. As he con-templated his next move, the general left behind his dead and wounded, many of whom had been lying exposed since May 19. Thus subjected to sun and heat, the bodies of the dead began to bloat and turn black—the stench became sickening. One Confederate soldier complained, "The Yanks are trying to stink us out of Vicksburg."

On May 25 white flags appeared along the Confederate line. Union soldiers hoped that the city would soon be surrendered. Their hopes were dashed as word quickly spread that Pemberton had written to Grant, imploring him "in the name of humanity" to bury his dead for the odor had become quite offensive. A truce was granted for two and one-half hours, dur-ing which time men in blue and gray mingled between the lines. "There a group of four played cards," recalled one sol-dier, "two Yanks and two Rebs, while others swapped tobacco for coffee." As the gruesome task of the burial details contin-ued, it appeared as if there was no war in progress. At the appointed time, however, the flags came down and everyone ran for cover. The siege of Vicksburg began.

9
LIFE UNDER SIEGE

Throughout the balance of May and into June Union soldiers slowly extended their lines to the left and right until they rimmed the beleaguered city. Once completed, the siege lines effectively isolated Pemberton's garrison, preventing all communication with the outside world. No supplies could reach the city. For the citizens and soldiers trapped in Vicksburg, life soon became a terrifying quest for survival. They had to subsist solely on what they had stockpiled. With each passing day supplies dwindled until nearly exhausted.

In order to conserve what food remained, Pemberton ordered the daily ration for his soldiers cut to three-quarters of the standard issue, then to half, then to a quarter. Rations were then cut again, and yet again, and yet again. By the end of June the garrison was issued only a handful of peas and rice per man per day. It was hardly enough to keep one alive, but it was all they had. Water, too, became a scarce commodi-

MARY LOUGHBOROUGH

Born in New York City in 1837, Mary Ann Webster moved with her family to St. Louis. Attractive and well educated, she married attorney James Loughborough in 1859. With the outbreak of the Civil War, the Loughboroughs were forced from St. Louis along with other pro-Southern Missourians, becoming refugees. James joined the Missouri State Guard and served on the staff of General Sterling Price; Mary followed him whenever she could. She found her way to Vicksburg only to be caught in the horrifying siege of 1863. The diary that she maintained during the trying ordeal was first published in 1864. *My Cave Life in Vicksburg* was an instant success, and remains one of the most widely quoted sources on life during the Siege of Vicksburg. After the war Mrs. Loughborough edited and published the periodical, *Southern Ladies Journal*, and wrote several other works, all while raising four children. She died in 1886.

ty and by late June had to be rationed.

Disease began to spread rapidly through the ranks. Dysentery, diarrhea, malaria, and various fevers all took a heavy toll of human life and offered a greater threat of death than did Union sharpshooters. As the siege progressed, a steady stream of men, first by the score, then by hundreds, could be seen to lay their weapons aside and walk or crawl as best they could to the hospitals in Vicksburg. Public buildings filled to capacity and many fine private residences were converted to hospitals. But there was little succor to be had as medicine, like food, was in short supply. Each day the "dead wagons" made the rounds. Bodies were brought out in ever increasing numbers and carried to the city cemetery north of town.

Adding to the horrors caused by shortages of food and water, Union land and naval batteries shelled the city relentlessly. Along the siege lines Federal artillerists placed 220 cannon, many of which were rifled guns, and bombarded the fortress city night and day. Admiral Porter also moved his gunboats into position to engage Confederate river batteries, stationing mortar scows on the far side of De Soto Point, opposite Vicksburg. Large 13-Inch mortars hurled 220-pound balls a half mile into the air, often blocking out the sun at the height of their trajectory. When the bombs, as they were called by the citizens of Vicksburg, crashed to earth the explosion created a crater almost fifteen feet deep. There appeared to be no place of safety anywhere.

Life under siege soon translated into life underground for citizens and soldiers alike as they dug deep into the hills, hollowing out rooms in which to live. Mary Loughborough, whose husband James was an officer in Pemberton's army, was forced underground with her daughter to seek shelter from the artillery projectiles that fell like rain upon the city. Of her experience she wrote:

The caves were plainly becoming a necessity, as some persons had been killed on the street by fragments of shells. The room that I had slept in had been struck by a fragment of a shell during the first night, and a large hole made in the ceiling. I shall never forget my extreme fear during the night, and my utter hopelessness of ever seeing the morning light. Terror stricken, we remained crouched in the cave, while shell after shell followed each other in quick succession. I endeavored by constant prayer to prepare myself for the sudden death I was almost certain awaited me. My heart stood still as we would hear the reports from the guns, and the rushing and fearful sound of the shell as it came toward us. As it neared, the noise became deafening; the air was full of the rushing sound; pains darted through my temples; my ears were full of the confusing noise; and, as it exploded, the report flashed through my head like an electric shock, leaving me in a quiet state of terror the most painful that I can imagine—cowering in a corner, holding my child to my heart—the only feeling of my life being the choking throbs of my heart, that rendered me almost breathless. As singly as they fell short, or beyond the cave, I was aroused by a feeling of thankfulness that was short of duration. Again and again the terrible fright came over us in that night.

"Caves were the fashion—the rage—over besieged Vicksburg," noted one terror-stricken resident. "Negroes, who understood their business, hired themselves out to dig them, at from thirty to fifty dollars, according to the size." Buying and selling of caves became a brisk and often lucrative business. One citizen explained, "Many persons, considering different localities unsafe, would sell them to others, who had been less fortunate, or less provident; and so great was the demand for cave workmen, that a new branch of industry sprang up and became popular."

Despite life in a cave, many of the townspeople remained defiant. Among them was Emma Balfour, who entered in her diary on May 30: "The general impression is that they fire at this city, in that way thinking that they will wear out the women and children and sick, and Gen. Pemberton will be impatient to surrender the place on that account, but they little know the spirit of the Vicksburg women and children if they expect this." A woman whose remarkable strength would be

EMMA BALFOUR

A prominent Vicksburg socialite whose 1862 Christmas ball was interrupted by the arrival of Federal gunboats, Emma Balfour became an astute observer of the war's impact on her city. Born in Virginia in 1818, she moved to Mississippi with her first husband and remained there after his death in 1844. Three years later she married Dr. William Balfour. During the spring and summer of 1863 she described in her diary the horrors of life and death under siege. With the rest of Vicksburg's inhabitants, she endured a six-week-long bombardment in a subterranean world of caves, cellars, and trenches, suffering disease and, eventually, starvation. Her diary offers some of the most vivid descriptions of this hellish existence available. Mrs. Balfour died at Ashville, North Carolina, in 1887. Her Vicksburg house became a tour home in which the Christmas ball is reenacted each year.

taxed to the limit, she boasted with pride, "Rather than let them know that they are causing us any suffering, I would be content to suffer martyrdom!"

Her sentiments were shared by many in the early days of siege; but as the bombardment continued day after weary day, week after bloody week, even the resolute began to weaken. Civilians soon realized that they were not immune to the death of the battlefield. Although figures varied as to the total of civilian casualties, the harsh reality was that innocent men, women, and children died victims of war. Mrs. Loughborough recorded in her journal the death of one child:

> Sitting in the cave, one evening, I heard the most heartrending screams and moans. I was told that a mother had taken a child into a cave about a hundred yards from us; and having laid it on its little bed, as the poor woman believed, in safety, she took her seat near the entrance of the cave. A mortar shell came rushing through the air, and fell with much force, entering the earth above the sleeping child—oh! most horrible sight to the mother— crushing in the upper part of the little sleeping head, and taking away the young innocent life without a look or word of passing love to be treasured in the mother's heart.

The dreaded bombs preyed on those in Vicksburg regardless of gender, race, or age. "A little negro child, playing in the yard, had found a shell;" recalled one resident. The discovery ended in death for the child, who "in rolling and turning it, had innocently pounded the fuse; the terrible explosion followed, showing as the white smoke floated away, the mangled remains of a life that to the mother's heart had possessed all of beauty and joy."

A Confederate soldier observed that the only time the shelling stopped was when Federal artillerists ate their morning, noon, and evening meals. During these brief intervals, when silence reigned supreme, many who lived in Vicksburg were lured into a false sense of security and ventured forth from their caves. Often they were trapped on the city streets when the shelling resumed and had to dodge the deadly projectiles as they raced for the shelter of the caves. Not all, however, reached safety. The observant Mrs. Loughborough captured one such tragedy:

> A young girl, becoming weary in the confinement of the cave, hastily ran to the house in the interval that elapsed between the slowly falling shells. On returning, an explosion sounded near her—one wild scream, and she ran into her mother's presence, sinking like a wounded dove, the life blood flowing over the light summer dress in crimson ripples from a death-wound in her side, caused by the shell fragment.

The sufferings of those in Vicksburg would haunt for the remainder of her days one woman who clung to life in the caves. "The screams of the women of Vicksburg were the saddest I have ever heard," she later wrote of those who lost loved ones to Union shells. "The wailings over the dead seemed full of heart-sick agony. I cannot attempt to describe the thrill of pity, mingled with fear, that pierced my soul, as suddenly vibrating through the air would come these sorrowful shrieks!—these pitiful moans!—sometimes almost simultaneously with the explosion of a shell."

During one of the more intense periods of shelling, Margaret Lord, wife of the Reverend Dr. William Lord, rector of Christ Church, tried to comfort her daughter Lida as the family crouched in the basement of their house of worship. "Don't cry

COONSKIN'S TOWER

On his approach to Vicksburg, Lieutenant Henry Foster of Company B, 23d Indiana Infantry, entered the Shirley House (on the Jackson Road, 400 yards from the Third Louisiana Redan) in search of souvenirs. He emerged with a coonskin cap, which he wore for the balance of the campaign. A noted sharpshooter, "Coonskin" Foster later built a tower out of railroad ties from which he could ply his trade during the siege. "Coonskin's Tower" became a popular attraction for Union soldiers who wanted a better look at the enemy's works. The tower was so popular that Foster began to charge twenty-five cents for admission. General Grant was a frequent visitor. One day on the tower, Grant recklessly exposed himself to harm as he examined the situation through his field glasses. A Confederate soldier spotted him, but did not fire. Instead he shouted obscenities, telling the unidentified man to get down or get shot. A Confederate officer noticed the commotion and recognized Grant, at which point he reprimanded his soldier, not for failing to fire but for using abusive language toward an officer—even if that officer was an enemy. Grant, recognizing the danger if not the insult, left the tower.

my darling," she soothed the child, assuring her that "God will protect us." The little girl could not be calmed. "But, momma, she said, "I's so 'fraid God's killed too!"

The shelling and constant fear of death wore as heavily on the nerves of soldiers in the trenches as it did on citizens such as Lida Lord. "Another day like the past twenty-one as one day could be like another," complained Lieutenant William Drennan in the pages of his diary on June 9, 1863. "Monotony does not convey all the sameness of these days imposes on one. There is a tension of nerves, an extreme anxiety, as you have experienced for a few moments and that you have felt—had you to endure it long, it would craze you." Two days later he wrote of the specter that overshadowed the monotony of events in Vicksburg and made the days so difficult to bear. "The mortality here at this time is very great; hardly a day passes but I see dozens of men carried to their last homes. They are buried in a trench with a blanket for a shroud. Coffins can not be had for all of them. Graves are dug today for use tomorrow."

Citizens and soldiers alike came to fear that death was certain should the siege continue throughout the summer. Everywhere they looked evidenced the destructive power of the besieging army, the grip of which was slowly strangling them into submission. "How blightingly the hand of warfare lay upon the town," observed Mary Loughborough, whose memory of life in the once magnificent city of Vicksburg seemed but a dream. Food supplies dwindled and, just as with the soldiers who stood steadfast in the trenches, the citizens of Vicksburg came to stare at starvation. Prices for all commodities were exorbitant as goods of any kind became practically nonexistent. By the end of June, one could walk through the market places along Washington Street and see skinned rats for sale. Shortages of even life's basic necessities were made painfully more apparent as the *Daily Citizen*, Vicksburg's leading newspaper, came to be issued on wallpaper.

Yet, in the midst of suffering and death, there was new life.

At least two children were born in caves during the siege. In honor of the circumstances that greeted his arrival into the world, one boy was christened William Siege Green. For the new-born babies, their parents, and all others in Vicksburg, there were also reasons for hope. Surely the authorities in Richmond would not forsake a city as significant as Vicksburg was to the Confederacy. Knowing that Joe Johnston had been sent to Mississippi by President Davis to rescue Vicksburg and its besieged garrison, Vicksburg's inhabitants prayed for deliverance.

10
To Rescue Gibraltar

The gas chandeliers at the president's house in Richmond burned well into the night as May turned into June. Jefferson Davis paced the floor as he directed that troops from as far away as the Atlantic coast be sent to Johnston. The president and Secretary of War James A. Seddon even contemplated sending General Robert E. Lee or some of his troops from the Army of Northern Virginia in a desperate attempt to save Vicksburg.

Having evacuated Jackson on May 14, Johnston's force marched northeast toward Canton, where the Virginian began to assemble the Army of Relief. Confederate troops soon poured into his camps from Tennessee and the Carolinas, swelling his numbers to 32,000 men by the first week in June. Including the 30,000-man garrison in Vicksburg, the armies of Pemberton and Johnston enjoyed numeric superiority over Grant. Such superiority of numbers would not last long as reinforcements were en route to Grant. Still, the situation offered the Confederates a window of opportunity to save Vicksburg through aggressive action. But neither Johnston nor Pemberton would accept the challenge.

In Vicksburg, the men in the trenches were confident that Joe Johnston would rescue them from the hands of Grant. Lieutenant Drennan entered in his diary on June 1, "I have every reason to believe that ten days will bring relief in the person of General Johnson [sic] and 50,000 men. God send him quickly." The belief expressed by the young lieutenant, one shared by many of his comrades in the Vicksburg defenses, slowly faded. Ten days later Drennen lamented, "I had fixed on the 10th of the month for General Johnson [sic] to come to our relief. But that day has come and gone and no relief in hearing as yet. I do not despair, by any means, yet I confess that I feel disheartened."

Each and every day the citizens and soldiers in Vicksburg strained their ears to hear the sounds of Johnston's liberating guns in the distance but, as the days of June slowly passed, there was no relief in hearing. "I think your movement should be made as soon as possible," Pemberton urged his superior. The Vicksburg commander, however, harbored little confidence that Johnston would move quickly or decisively and queried of him, "What aid am I to expect from you?" Johnston's answer was painfully terse: "I am too weak to save Vicksburg." Both the president and members of the Cabinet pleaded with Johnston to move, none more forcefully than Secretary of War Seddon, who admonished, "Vicksburg must not be lost without a desperate struggle. The interest and honor of the Confederacy forbid it." Nothing, however, could stir Johnston into action.

Desperate to save Vicksburg, President Davis and his advisors looked to Confederate forces in the vast Trans-Mississippi Department as a possible source of relief for the besieged garrison. Although Federal forces were active at various points

RICHARD TAYLOR

Born Kentucky 1826; son of President and Mexican War hero Zachary Taylor and brother-in-law of Confederate President Jefferson Davis; studied at Yale; became a successful sugar planter in Louisiana; elected colonel 9th Louisiana Infantry at the outbreak of the Civil War and went with the regiment to Virginia, arriving too late for First Manassas; promoted to brigadier general 1861; commanded the Louisiana Brigade in Major General Thomas J. "Stonewall" Jackson's Shenandoah Valley Campaign of 1862; present but not active during the Seven Days' Battles before Richmond; promoted to major general and assigned to command the District of Western Louisiana in 1862; unsuccessfully opposed Major General Nathaniel P. Banks' Bayou Teche Expedition in 1863, but turned back Banks' Red River Expedition the following spring; after a heated exchange in which he criticized his commander, General E. Kirby Smith, for not following up this success, he asked to be relieved; he was, however, promoted to lieutenant general and assigned to command the Department of Alabama, Mississippi, and East Louisiana; following the disaster at Nashville, he temporarily succeeded General John B. Hood in command of the Army of Tennessee, most of which he forwarded to the Carolinas to oppose Major General William

T. Sherman's advance; after the fall of Mobile he surrendered the last remaining Confederate force east of the Mississippi to Major General E.R.S. Canby on May 4, 1865; following the war he was active in Democratic politics and vigorously opposed Reconstruction policies; died at New York in 1879. That year he published *Destruction and Reconstruction*, one of the finest participant memoirs to be produced. Without any formal military training, General Taylor proved to be a most able commander. The Confederate repulse of the Red River Expedition, though largely overlooked, was a major achievement.

throughout his department, Lieutenant General E. Kirby Smith directed Major General Richard Taylor into Madison Parish, opposite the Mississippi River from Vicksburg, to attack the Union supply enclaves at Milliken's Bend and Young's Point in the mistaken belief that Grant depended on these bases to supply his army. But, by this time, Grant had established overland supply routes and the bases were lightly guarded by only a small number of white troops and some recently-recruited black regiments. Taylor opposed the idea and later wrote that "Remonstrances were to no avail. I was informed that all the Confederate authorities in the east were urgent for some effort on our part in behalf of Vicksburg, and that public opinion would condemn us if we did not *try to do something.*"

In obeyance of his orders, on June 5 Taylor rode into Richmond, Louisiana, where he was briefed on the disposition of Union troops along the Mississippi River. The following day, Major General John G. Walker's Texas Division, more than 4,000-strong, tramped into town. Taylor was anxious to strike immediately. He planned to hurl Walker's men against the Federal bases at Milliken's Bend and Young's Point, while a combat patrol led by Colonel Frank Bartlett of the 13th Louisiana Cavalry Battalion attacked the Union enclave at Lake Providence, farther north. In preparation for the assault, the Texans were permitted to rest for several hours and instructed to cook rations.

The Confederate plan of attack called for a night march. Shouldering their muskets, the Texans left Richmond at 6 p.m. on June 6, hoping to arrive at the Federal camps by sunrise. One Texan recalled the march:

> In sections four abreast, and close order, the troops took up the line of march, in anticipation of meeting almost certain death, but with undaunted, unquailing spirits. In breathless silence, with the high glittering stars looking

down upon them, through dark and deep
defiles marched the dense array of men, moving steadily forward; not a whisper was
heard—no sound of clanking saber, or rattle of
canteen and cup.

At Oak Grove plantation the road forked, the left fork led to
Milliken's Bend, the right to Young's Point. Walker sent
Brigadier General Henry McCulloch's Brigade toward Milliken's
Bend and Brigadier General James M. Hawes' Brigade toward
Young's Point, while he remained at Oak Grove with one
brigade in reserve.

McCulloch's Brigade arrived within a mile and a half of
Milliken's Bend at 2:30 a.m., when it was fired upon by Federal
pickets. Quickly deploying his troops into line of battle, the
Texan advanced astride the Richmond Road, driving the
Federals from one hedgerow to another. Once past the
hedgerows, McCulloch reformed his brigade within twenty-five
paces of the main Federal line. Shouting "No quarter for the
officers, kill the damned abolitionists, spare the niggers," the
Texans scaled the levee and closed on their enemy.

A withering volley stunned the Confederates, but the
untested black troops were unable to reload their cumbersome
weapons before the Texans were upon them. McCulloch reported that "The line was formed under a heavy fire from the
enemy, and the troops charged the breastworks, carrying it
instantly, killing and wounding many of the enemy by their
deadly fire, as well as the bayonet." The brigadier noted, "This
charge was resisted by the negro portion of the enemy's force
with considerable obstinacy, while the white or true Yankee
portion ran like whipped curs almost as soon as the charge
was ordered."

The Texans freely employed clubbed muskets and bayonets
as they surged over the cotton-bale barricades atop the levee.
Joseph P. Blessington of the 16th Texas recalled that "The

enemy gave away and stampeded pell-mell over the levee, in great terror and confusion. Our troops followed after them, bayoneting them by hundreds." Sweeping through the Federal encampment, McCulloch's men raced toward the second levee next to the river. Their efforts to cross, however, were driven

HENRY McCULLOCH

Born Tennessee 1816; moved to Texas in 1837; sheriff of Gonzales County, Texas; fought in several actions against Indians; commanded a company of Texas Rangers in the Mexican War; elected to the state legislature in 1853 and to the state senate two years later; appointed U.S. marshal for the eastern district of Texas in 1859; upon the secession of Texas, he received a Confederate commission as colonel; organized the 1st Texas Mounted Rifles to seize U.S. posts on the northwest Texas frontier and to protect the frontier from Indian attacks; briefly commanded the Confederate Department of Texas in 1861; afterward he headed a succession of districts and sub-districts in Texas; he was instrumental in assembling and forwarding troops for service outside the state; brigadier general 1862; in his only major combat action, McCulloch led a brigade at Milliken's Bend during the Vicksburg Campaign of 1863; his poor showing in handling a large body of troops brought a swift return to Texas; although he later commanded the important Northern Sub-district of Texas, his duties remained largely administrative; after the war he engaged in farming and ranching in Guadalupe County and was the superintendent of the Texas Asylum for the Deaf and Dumb; he died at Rockport, Texas, in 1895. Although he fared poorly as a combat commander, General McCulloch was a talented and useful administrator. His brother, Confederate General Ben McCulloch, was killed at Elkhorn Tavern, Arkansas, in 1862.

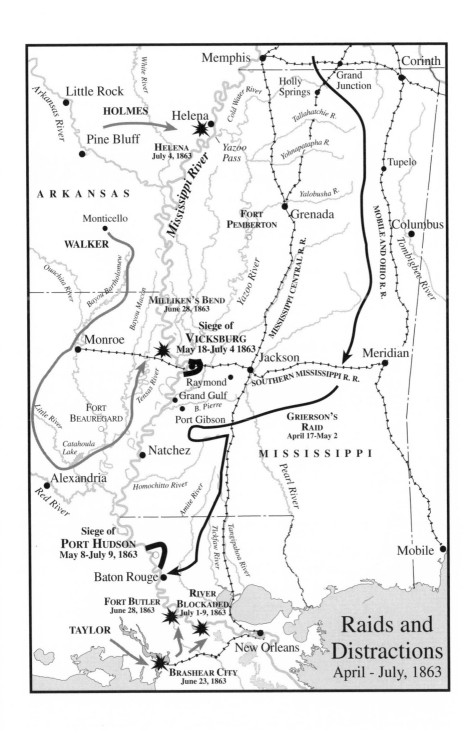

Raids and Distractions
April - July, 1863

back repeatedly by the rapid fire of the powerful Union iron-clad *Choctaw*, which supported the base.

Unable to cross the levee, the Texans eliminated isolated pockets of resistance and plundered the Federal camp. McCulloch sent an urgent request to Walker for reinforcements but, before help arrived, he spotted another gunboat, *Lexington*, moving upriver. Realizing that his troops were no match for gunboats, and without waiting for Walker's arrival, McCulloch ordered a withdrawal to Oak Grove plantation.

In the engagement at Milliken's Bend, McCulloch's Brigade suffered 44 killed, 131 wounded, and 10 missing, but inflicted 652 casualties, of which number 101 were killed, 285 wounded, and 266 missing. The lesser actions at Young's Point and Lake Providence also ended in failure for the Confederates. The bases remained in Federal possession throughout the siege.

In all probability, Confederate operations in Louisiana, initiated at this late date and with insufficient force, held little hope of impacting substantially the situation across the river. Perhaps an earlier effort could have made a difference, but too much time had been lost—time that Grant used to solidify his position and establish other supply routes.

In Mississippi, Joe Johnston's efforts to rescue Pemberton and the Vicksburg garrison would also be too little, too late. The window of opportunity presented to General Johnston by the numeric superiority of the combined Confederate forces in early June was permitted to close. Despite prodding from the authorities in Richmond and the clamor for action from the press, the general on whom the hopes of the Southern people rested would not move. He only complained of his lack of men, horses, wagons, artillery, and supplies, and offered an array of excuses for inactivity. According to Pemberton biographer Michael Ballard, "Johnston never had any intention of trying to save Vicksburg or its defenders. As usual when a bold, offensive maneuver was necessary, Johnston found every excuse not to move."

Aware that Johnston was massing troops with which to raise the siege, Grant requested reinforcements of his own. Responding with alacrity, Washington authorities ordered troops from Kentucky, Tennessee, Missouri, and Arkansas to move quickly to Vicksburg. Veterans of the IX Corps, who had fought at Antietam, Fredericksburg, and on a score of other battlefields in the East, arrived in mid-June under the command of Major General John Grubb Parke. From Memphis came elements of the XVI Corps under Major General Cadwallader C. Washburn and the Provisional Division of Brigadier General Nathan Kimball, while the division of Major General Francis J. Herron came from west of the Mississippi River to augment Union forces around Vicksburg.

The bulk of these troops were used to establish what became known as the "Exterior Line." Running east from Haynes' Bluff, overlooking the Yazoo River north of Vicksburg, to Oak Ridge, then south to the railroad bridge across Big Black River east of town, the line was manned by 34,000 troops and supported by 72 guns, all under Sherman's personal command. It was a formidable array of veteran soldiers, whose mission was to keep Johnston at arm's length. Although Confederate cavalry probed the line for weakness, none was discovered and Sherman's troops safeguarded the rear of Grant's besieging army.

Finally, on the morning of July 1, Johnston ordered his troops west toward Vicksburg. Under the scorching sun, the soldiers straggled badly, suffering from the thick clouds of dust that rose from the road. Approaching Big Black River on July 3, Johnston recognized that it would be impossible to force a crossing of the river in the face of Sherman's army. But by then it was immaterial. The Union cannon that for weeks had rained death on the fortress city ceased fire. Ominous silence settled over the region, indicating that for the garrison of Vicksburg time had run out.

11

UNVEXED TO THE SEA

Throughout the siege Union soldiers dug approaches toward the Confederate line. Forming zigzags and then parallels, Grant's infantry and artillery moved first to within 300 yards, then 200 yards, then only 100 yards from the city's defenses. The digging continued as Union soldiers worked their way up to the parapets of Vicksburg. The object was to get as close as possible to the Confederate fortifications so that if an attack was ordered all they need do was pour out of their trench, scale the parapet, and fall among the enemy. This would minimize casualties and maximize troop strengths, allowing the attackers to hit the Confederates with enough force to seize the forts and gain access to Vicksburg. An alternative approach was to tunnel underneath the enemy works, hollow out galleries, fill them with black powder, and destroy the Confederate fortifications with a massive explosion.

Union soldiers excavated thirteen approaches at different

points along the siege line in order to mine the Confederate works. Of these, the most successful was known as "Logan's Approach." Stationed along the Jackson Road, men of John Logan's Division inched their way toward the Third Louisiana Redan, cutting a sap, or trench, that was seven feet deep and eight feet wide. Union fatigue parties, working at first behind the shelter of a railroad flatcar stacked with bales of cotton, reached the redan on June 23. The soldiers carved a gallery directly under the fort and prepared it for mining.

The Confederates inside the Third Louisiana Redan knew exactly what their enemy was doing and sank countershafts from behind their own lines, hoping to locate the tunnel and destroy the mine before it could be detonated. In the counter-shafts, which ranged from fifteen to twenty feet in depth, the air was stifling, making it next to impossible to breathe. At the bottom of the countershafts, however, the Confederates could hear the sounds of Federal soldiers digging opposite them. They could even make out their conversations. But sounds traveled differently under ground than they did on the surface and the Confederates could not tell from which direction or from what distance the sounds came. All they knew was that on June 25 the digging opposite them stopped, which meant only one thing—the mine had been completed.

That day Federal soldiers packed 2,200 pounds of black powder into the mine. Grant, who had set 3 p.m. as the time for detonation, arrived on the Jackson Road and ordered the fuse lit. Tense moments passed as the Federals waited to storm into the breach and seize Vicksburg. But 3 o'clock came and went—no explosion. Minutes passed, 3:05, 3:10, 3:15, still nothing. Tension turned to anxiety as the troops wondered when "volunteers" would be ordered in to find the problem.

Suddenly at 3:28, there was a muffled thud, then a loud explosion as the ground began to break apart. Inside the column of flame and dirt that shot to the air observers could see men, mules, and accouterments flying skyward. Before the dust could even settle, Union soldiers poured into the crater and attempted to exploit the breach. In the wild melee that ensued, soldiers from both armies fought wildly with clubbed muskets and bayonets, and tossed hand grenades back and forth. The battle raged in unabated fury for twenty-six hours as Grant threw in one fresh regiment after another, all to no avail. As the crater filled with the bodies of the dead and wounded, Confederate Colonel Eugene Erwin led his 6th Missouri Infantry forward in a desperate attempt to drive back the enemy. Erwin, the grandson of Henry Clay, was cut down as his men slammed into the Federals and at the point of bayonet sealed the breach. Grant's great gamble had failed and, with little alternative, he recalled his troops.

Undaunted, the Federals on July 1 planted and detonated a second mine that held 1,800 pounds of powder. But this time no infantry assault followed. As the mine was readied, the Southerners pressed into service eight black men, who were placed in the countershafts to work under the direction of a corporal. When the mine was detonated, the men in the countershafts were buried alive. One, however, a slave named Abraham, was blown skyward and fell to earth behind Union lines. Remarkably, though he landed on his head, he was unhurt. Union soldiers ran to him, picked him up, and dusted him off. One soldier even had the audacity to ask him, "How high did you go?" to which he replied, "Dunno...but t'ink about t'ree mile." Abraham was placed in a tent by some enterprising soldiers, who charged admission for others to see "the man who was blown to freedom."

That day, Grant was notified by his subordinates that given just a few more days of digging, thirteen mines could be planted and detonated simultaneously. This was the moment Grant and his army had been working toward all the many weeks of the siege. The Confederates likely could not have withstood such an attack. But the assault never came. On Friday, July 3, as Grant planned an attack for the following Monday, white flags appeared on the parapets of Vicksburg and firing along the lines ceased.

The citizens of Vicksburg and their Confederate defenders were puzzled by the quiet of the morning. Their pride, hopes, and dreams would not permit them to accept the stillness as the end. But it was. The fate of their city and their nation would soon be decided. At 10 a.m. General Bowen and Lieutenant Colonel Louis Montgomery of Pemberton's staff rode out from the besieged city. With soldierly bearing they performed their humiliating task, delivering a letter that requested an armistice in order to arrange terms for the capitulation of Vicksburg.

Pemberton's decision to surrender was based on the consensus of his division commanders, whose men had reached the limits of human endurance. In response to a circular in which the commanding general inquired about the condition of

ABRAHAM

Abraham was among several slaves pressed into service by the Confederates to dig countershafts in an effort to thwart Federal mining activities beneath the Vicksburg defenses. When Union soldiers detonated a mine under the Third Louisiana Redan on July 1, the slaves were buried alive, except for Abraham, who was blown skyward, landing within the Union lines. Somehow, Abraham escaped the ordeal unhurt and was introduced to Generals Grant and McPherson. Something of a celebrity, he was placed on display in a tent by some enterprising soldiers, who charged their curious comrades fifty cents for a look at the man who survived the mine explosion and his flight to freedom.

the troops and their ability to cut through the siege lines, his officers recommended that "an immediate proposition be made to capitulate." Although the soldiers themselves still managed a lighthearted verbal exchange with the enemy, warning them to "look out as we have a new general...General Starvation," a letter handed to Pemberton better reflected the desperate nature of the situation within the army. Entitled "Appeal for help," the letter implored, "If you can't feed us, you had better surrender us, horrible as the idea is, than suffer this noble army to disgrace themselves by desertion." The document was signed "MANY SOLDIERS."

Despairing of relief, Pemberton's own preference was to place himself at the head of his army and make a desperate attempt to cut through the lines. He knew that such a desperate action was his "only hope of saving [himself] from shame and disgrace." The commander, though, submitted to a higher sense of honor, acknowledging that "my duty is to sacrifice myself to save the army which has so nobly done its duty to defend Vicksburg."

After long debate and agonized thought, Pemberton informed his officers that "I therefore concur with you and shall offer to surrender this army on the 4th of July." As a Northerner, he believed that he might obtain favorable terms on July 4. "I know my people," he told his subordinates. "To gratify their national vanity they would yield then what could not be extorted from them at any other time." With this in mind he opened communications with Grant.

Grant's response was characteristically blunt: "The useless effusion of blood you propose stopping by this course can be ended at any time you may choose, by an unconditional surrender of the city and garrison." Indeed, Grant was the master of the situation. He had fought too long and too hard to accept anything less than unconditional surrender. These terms he owed to himself and to his army.

In the company of his generals, Pemberton received Grant's

answer. He had hoped for more favorable terms, terms to which he believed the valiant defenders of Vicksburg were entitled. But all hopes were dashed as he read the note. "Reduced to the ignominy that awaits a defeated leader," the Confederate commander prepared to meet Grant later in the day to discuss the capitulation of Vicksburg.

Shortly before 3 p.m. all was astir along the Jackson Road. White flags of truce once again appeared along the Confederate works and firing quickly came to a halt. From the east came a group of horsemen led by Grant. "It was a glorious sight to officers and soldiers on the line where these white flags were visible," he wrote, "and the news soon spread to all parts of the command." Expressing a belief shared by the soldiers, he continued, "The troops felt that their long and weary marches, hard fighting, ceaseless watching by day and night, in a hot climate, exposure to all sorts of weather, to disease, and, worst of all, to the gibes of many Northern papers that came to them saying all their suffering was in vain, that Vicksburg would never be taken, were at last at an end and the Union sure to be saved."

From the west rode three Confederate officers, among them General Pemberton. The ride from his headquarters to the front lines was the longest one ever made by the general and those with him. These men were slowed in their journey, for the road out from Vicksburg was "hideously gashed and gutted" from Union artillery fire. They shared few words as they rode toward destiny, but those with Pemberton heard him say, "I feel a confidence that I shall stand justified to my government, if not to the Southern people…should it be otherwise—the consolation of having done the only thing which in my opinion could give security to Vicksburg and the surrounding country…will be reward enough." The consolation of which he spoke was soon to be his only reward.

The Confederate horsemen rode out beyond their works and dismounted. Walking forward they met the Union officers and shook hands. Grant recalled, "Pemberton and I had served in the same division during part of the Mexican War. I knew him very well, therefore, and greeted him as an old acquaintance." Nothing, however, could put the Confederate commander at ease and he appeared "much excited." Pemberton immediately inquired of Grant his terms for the capitulation of Vicksburg. Grant had no terms other than immediate and unconditional surrender, to which the Southern commander replied, "Then, sir, it is unnecessary that you and I should hold any further conversation; we will go to fighting again at once." As he turned to leave, Pemberton pointed a finger at Grant and stressed, "I can assure you general that you will bury many more of your men before you enter Vicksburg."

In hopes that the surrender could be consummated, Grant proposed a conference among the subordinates present to discuss surrender terms. The two commanders then walked a short distance and, in the shade of a stunted oak, sat and reminisced about their days in Mexico while aides arranged for a cease-fire and provided Grant with time to reconsider his terms for the surrender of Vicksburg.

Rumors spread like wildfire throughout the city and among the soldiers of both armies. Conjectures varied, but it was commonly believed that surrender had been decided upon. Captain George H. Hynds of the 31st Tennessee Infantry wrote, "I believe we have been sold and Pemberton is now giving the bill of sale for us and receiving his reward." He added ruefully, "It is hard to be sold and not get part of the purchase money." Surrender held no appeal for Lieutenant Drennan either: "Oh! It is heart-sickening, for should Vicksburg be surrendered and we be taken prisoners," he wrote, "I have no idea that we shall see outside prison walls for months—perhaps not during the war. A prison has no charms for me and I still hope that they parole."

The afternoon was oppressively hot. At 5 p.m. the last gun was fired in defense of Vicksburg. Chaplain Foster of the 35th

Mississippi recalled, "I heard the shrill note of the artillery-man's bugle. It was the first time I heard the blast of the bugle during the siege. In a moment our canon (sic) ceased firing. The enemy beyond the river also ceased and stillness again rested upon the peaceful bosom of the father of waters."

After weeks of almost constant firing, the soldiers of both armies found the silence unnatural. To Lieutenant Richard L. Howard of the 124th Illinois, "The silence began to be fearfully oppressive. For so many long days and nights it had been a continuous battle. Not a minute but the crack of the rifle or the boom of the cannon had been in our ears. And much of the time it had been deafening. Now it was still, absolutely still. ...It was leaden. We could not bear it; it settled down so close; it hugged us with its hollow, unseen arms till we could scarcely breathe." Chaplain Foster bore witness that throughout Vicksburg "a painful silence, foreboding evil, reigns over the doomed city."

Vicksburg was a doomed city. Grant recalled, "When I returned to my headquarters I sent for all the corps and division commanders with the army immediately confronting Vicksburg...I informed them of the contents of Pemberton's letter, of my reply and the substance of the interview, and that I was ready to hear any suggestions." Although he favored an unconditional surrender, Grant understood that this would tie up Union land and naval forces until the prisoners could be transported northward to prison. After conferring with his chief subordinates, he decided simply to parole the garrison. Thus spared a prison term, the Confederates would sign a parole, promising not to take up arms against the Federal government until properly exchanged.

These would be welcome terms to Pemberton and his weary soldiers as morale had been virtually destroyed by the length and hardships of the siege. To help expedite the process, Grant directed that during night Federal pickets should communicate to their Confederate counterparts his intention "to parole all officers and men, and permit them to go home" should Pemberton surrender. Grant understood that many Confederate soldiers would be quick to accept this generous offer and leave for home shortly after the city capitulated.

True to his word, at 10 p.m. Grant sent in his final, amended terms. Pemberton read the letter and, without comment, submitted it to a council of his generals. Pemberton would later write that "My own inclination was to reject these terms." His generals, however, favored acceptance. Pemberton replied: "In the main your terms are accepted; but in justice both to the honor and spirit of my troops, manifested in the defense of Vicksburg, I have to submit the following amendment, which if acceded to by you, will perfect the agreement between us." He proposed to evacuate the works around Vicksburg at 10 a.m. and to surrender the city and garrison "by marching out with my colors and arms, stacking them in front of my present lines, after which you will take possession."

Midnight had passed by the time Pemberton received Grant's reply: the amendment could not be acceded to in full. Tiring of the exchange, Grant warned the Confederate general that "Should no notification be received of your acceptance of my terms by 9 a.m., I shall regard them as having been rejected, and shall act accordingly."

Enough blood had been shed in defense of Vicksburg. In the early morning hours Pemberton sent his acceptance to Grant, writing "I have the honor to acknowledge the receipt of your communication of this day, and in reply to say that terms proposed by you are accepted." It was finished. The surrender of the fortress city and its garrison was consummated. Vicksburg had fallen and with it went all hopes of Southern independence.

On the morning of July 4, 1863, white flags fluttered in the breeze above the city's fortifications. Marching out from their works, Confederate soldiers furled their flags, stacked their arms, and turned over their accouterments, at which time the victorious Union army marched in and took possession of

Vicksburg—the Gibraltar on the Mississippi River that had eluded them for so long.

Grant rode into Vicksburg along Jackson Road and down to the Warren County Courthouse. There he watched as the Stars and Stripes were unfurled atop the building. He then rode down to the waterfront, where he personally thanked and congratulated Admiral Porter for the assistance rendered by the United States Navy during the campaign for Vicksburg. Almost as an afterthought, he sent a message to Washington, informing President Lincoln of the city's surrender. It took three days for the message to reach the capital. Two days later, on July 9, the only remaining Confederate bastion on the Mississippi River, Port Hudson, Louisiana, fell into Union hands. Some two weeks later, upon learning that the unarmed steamboat *Imperial* had reached New Orleans from St. Louis, Lincoln wrote "Thank God," and declared that "The Father of Waters again goes unvexed to the sea."

EPILOGUE

Martial music echoed through the streets of Vicksburg as columns of Union infantry with colors waving converged on the Warren County Courthouse on July 4, 1863. Church bells pealed a thunderous ovation and the heavy tread of troops in steady cadence reverberated among the buildings. Adding to the medley of sounds were the high-pitched steam whistles of the Union fleet as Admiral Porter's gunboats, gaily bedecked with flags fluttering in the breeze, rounded to along the city's waterfront.

A crowd assembled around the courthouse and watched with mixed emotions as the Confederate flag, which had flown from the cupola as a symbol of defiance, was lowered and replaced by the Stars and Stripes. Tears flowed down the cheeks of the vanquished and the newly liberated alike. But when the music stopped and the crowd dispersed, one fact was clear—Vicksburg was now an occupied city and, with the surrender of Port Hudson on July 9, the Mississippi River was once again open to navigation.

The significance of this event was recognized immediately across the nation. In the North, newspapers heralded the triumph as one of the war's great victories. Some even claimed that it was the most decisive campaign ever waged in American military history—and justly so. In a period of only 13 weeks, Grant's army had inflicted more than 9,000 battle casualties, and upon the surrender of Vicksburg, captured 172 pieces of artillery, 50,000 shoulder weapons, and 29,491 officers and men—a staggering combination of men and material that the South could not replace. Demonstrating that he was one of history's great battle captains, Grant had accomplished this remarkable feat while suffering the loss of only 10,142 men killed, wounded, and missing.

Throughout the South, people viewed the loss of Vicksburg as the death knell of the Confederacy. In addition to the loss of the garrison and its war material, the South was now split in two along the line of the Mississippi River, the vital supply routes that linked the Confederate heartland to the vast Trans-Mississippi region severed. Coupled with the Federal blockade of Southern ports on the Atlantic and Gulf coasts, that eventually slowed to a trickle the arrival of essential war materials from Europe on which the armies of Robert E. Lee and Braxton Bragg relied, the South was virtually isolated. Now trapped in the coils of the giant anaconda, as old General Scott had envisioned, the Confederacy could not long endure.

The summer of 1863 marked a turning point in the American Civil War as across the broad spectrum of conflict the armies of the North and South clashed in bloody combat. In Mississippi, Tennessee, Virginia, and Pennsylvania the lifeblood of a nation was poured out upon the earth as brothers fought one another in defense of ideals held dear. As Grant slowly established his lines around Vicksburg, the Confederate Army of Northern Virginia, under the redoubtable Lee, pushed northward across Maryland and into Pennsylvania. The campaign on which so many Southern hopes rested, climaxed in a titanic three-day struggle at Gettysburg, during which more than 51,000 soldiers, Union and Confederate, became casualties of war. On the day that Vicksburg fell, Lee's defeated army began its bitter retreat from Gettysburg—a shadow of its former self. Reflecting on the turn of events in July 1863, Colonel Josiah Gorgas, chief of the Confederate Ordnance Bureau, lamented, "Yesterday we rode on the pinnacle of success—today absolute ruin seems to be our portion. The Confederacy totters to its destruction." Twenty-one months later, the inevitability of Appomattox Court House ended the greatest tragedy in American history.

For those who experienced victory and defeat on the fields of Mississippi and Louisiana, and on the waters of the great river, the Vicksburg Campaign became a defining event.

Although most of the Confederate officers and men, once paroled and exchanged, would fight again, some would never recover from the ordeal. The valiant John Bowen contracted dysentery during the siege and died only days after the surrender.

John Pemberton's career as a general officer was over. Disgraced, he resigned his commission, but returned to duty as a lieutenant colonel, and faithfully served his adopted country to the very end. In 1917 the United States government erected a monument to John Pemberton on the grounds of Vicksburg National Military Park, which is more than can be said for Joe Johnston, Braxton Bragg, or a host of other Confederate generals who met with defeat during the Civil War.

Joe Johnston, who in truth abandoned the Vicksburg garrison, avoided the ignominy that Pemberton shouldered. He refused to accept any blame for the loss and remained a popular figure in the Confederacy. His strategic withdrawal in the face of Sherman's advance on Atlanta in 1864 was masterful, but resulted in his removal from command, when again he refused to fight for a strategically important city.

The successful conquest of Vicksburg would have a profound impact on the Federal army, its command structure, and how it would prosecute the war to conclusion. The long campaign confirmed many a general's credentials, resurrected troubled careers, and brought new leaders to the forefront. But not all would enjoy victory's rewards. John McClernand, the crusty and ambitious commander of the Union XIII Corps, ran afoul of Grant and was relieved of his command at Vicksburg on June 18, 1863. Although he was eventually restored to command in 1864 and led the XIII Corps during the latter stage of the ill-fated Red River Campaign, his military career was over. He returned to the arena of politics, but never again exercised the influence he once held in Congress. McClernand died in 1900, having lived to see the field of his most stirring triumph and stinging defeat turned into a national military park, on the grounds of which the people of Illinois erected a magnificent equestrian statue in his honor. Ironically, there are no monuments on the hallowed ground at Vicksburg to honor either McPherson or Sherman, the corps commanders on whom Grant lavished credit for the victory.

For many others, though, Vicksburg brought plaudits and promotion. Like McClernand, John Logan and Frank Blair demonstrated boldly the potential of civilian or "political" generals. Both rose to command corps and played significant roles in the war's closing campaigns. Logan temporarily led the Army of the Tennessee in July 1864, rallying it to victory in the Battle of Atlanta after James McPherson was killed in action.

McPherson, the young, handsome, and personable commander of the XVII Corps, received the praise of Grant and Sherman for his actions during the Vicksburg Campaign and was promoted to brigadier general in the Regular Army. Yet, the inexperience and timidity he demonstrated on the fields at Raymond and Champion Hill surfaced on other fields. He rose to command the Army of the Tennessee, but never justified the confidence that his superiors had in him. At Atlanta in 1864, he became the only Union army commander killed during the Civil War.

No man other than Grant benefitted more from the triumph at Vicksburg than William T. Sherman. Grant's chief subordinate, he succeeded his friend as commander of the Army of the Tennessee and shared in the victories at Chattanooga. He understood the totality of war to a greater degree than most of his contemporaries. Recognizing that the morale of civilians who supported armed resistance to the government must be crushed in order to end the rebellion, Sherman would implement his concept of total war in the Meridian Campaign in February 1864. With Grant's promotion to overall command of the Federal armies, Sherman assumed direction of the war in the West. After capturing Atlanta, he continued his total war approach as he pushed through Georgia on his "March to the Sea." Thus, while in Virginia, Grant defeated Lee, in Mississippi, Georgia, and the Carolinas, Sherman conquered the South. Promoted to lieutenant general in 1866, he followed Grant as commanding general of the army in 1869, becoming only the second man in American history to wear four stars. With the exception of George Washington, Sherman is perhaps the best known American soldier. Therefore, it is ironic that there are no monuments to Sherman on any of the battlefields on which he fought during the Civil War.

Vicksburg made Ulysses S. Grant and in so doing gave Lincoln a man who could lead the Federal armies to ultimate victory. Proving his critics wrong, Grant finally gained the recognition he had earned. He won spectacular victories at Chattanooga in November 1863, and the following March received promotion to lieutenant general in command of all Union armies. Battling his way to the gates of Richmond and Petersburg, he compelled Lee to evacuate the Confederate capital and, at Appomattox Courthouse on April 9, 1865, he received the surrender of yet another Southern army. Although Grant later served two terms as president of the United States, he is best remembered for his service as a general during the Civil War. Throughout his life, he remained a plain, unassuming man of impeccable honesty, loyal to his family, his country, and his fellow soldiers. In 1885 Grant, fighting a losing battle with throat cancer, raced to finish his memoirs—the sale of which would leave his family financially secure. In the manuscript, completed just before his death, he wrote, "These volumes are dedicated to the American soldier and sailor."

In February 1899, Vicksburg National Military Park was established by the Congress to commemorate the great campaign. Today, the park encompasses 1,800 acres, including the grounds of Vicksburg National Cemetery, and boasts 1,324 monuments, markers, tablets, and plaques, making Vicksburg one of the world's more densely monumented battlefields. The magnificent sculptures of stone and bronze that dot the landscape make it, in the words of one Civil War veteran, "the art park of the world." It is truly a fitting memorial to the soldiers and sailors in blue and gray who struggled throughout the area during the campaigns of 1862 and 1863. Their service is best recalled in the words inscribed on the Pennsylvania Monument:

Here brothers died for their principles;
Here heroes died for their country;
and a united people will forever cherish the
precious legacy of their noble manhood.

APPENDIX A

ORGANIZATION OF CONFEDERATE FORCES

ARMY OF VICKSBURG
LT. GEN. JOHN C. PEMBERTON

STEVENSON'S DIVISION
MAJ. GEN. CARTER L. STEVENSON

1ST BRIGADE
BRIG. GEN. SETH BARTON
40th Georgia, Col. Abda Johnson, Lt. Col. Robert M. Young
41st Georgia, Col. William E. Curtiss
42d Georgia, Col. Robert J. Henderson
43d Georgia, Col. Skidmore Harris (k), Capt. Mathadeus M. Grantham
52d Georgia, Col. Charles D. Phillips (m), Maj. John J. Moore
Pettus Flying Artillery, Lt. Milton H. Trantham
Company A, Pointe Coupee Artillery, Lt. John Yoist
Company C, Pointe Coupee Artillery, Capt. Alexander Chust

2D BRIGADE
BRIG. GEN. ALFRED CUMMING
34th Georgia, Col. James A.W. Johnson
36th Georgia, Col. Jesse A. Glenn, Maj. Charles E. Broyles
39th Georgia, Col. Joseph T. McConnel (w), Lt. Col. J.F.B. Jackson
56th Georgia, Col. Elihu P. Watkins (w), Lt. Col. John T. Slaughter
57th Georgia, Lt. Col. Cincinnatus S. Guyton, Col. William Barkuloo
Cherokee Georgia Artillery, Capt. Max Van Den Corput

3D BRIGADE
BRIG. GEN. EDWARD D. TRACY (K)
COL. ISHAM W. GARROTT*
BRIG. GEN. STEPHEN D. LEE
20th Alabama, Col. Isham W. Garrott (k), Col. Edmund W. Pettus
23d Alabama, Col. Franklin K. Beck
30th Alabama, Col. Sharles M. Shelley, Capt. John C. Francis
31st Alabama, Col. Daniel R. Hundley (w), Lt. Col. Thomas M. Arrington,
Maj. George W. Mathieson

46th Alabama, Col. Michael L. Woods (c), Capt. George E. Brewer

Waddell's Alabama Battery, Capt. James F. Waddell

*Garrott was killed on June 7, 1863. His commission as a brigadier general, dated May 28, 1863, arrived after his death.

4TH BRIGADE
COL. ALEXANDER W. REYNOLDS

3d Tennessee (Provisional Army), Col. Newton J. Lillard

31st Tennessee, Col. William M. Bradford

43d Tennessee, Col. James W. Gillespie

59th Tennessee, Col. William L. Eaken

3d Maryland Battery, Capt. Fred O. Claiborne (k), Capt. John B. Rowan

WAUL'S TEXAS LEGION
COL. THOMAS N. WAUL

1st Infantry Battalion, Maj. Eugene S. Bolling

2d Infantry Battalion, Lt. Col. James Wrigley

Zouave Battalion, Capt. J.B. Fleitas

Cavalry Detachment, Lt. Thomas J. Cleveland

Artillery Company, Capt. J.Q. Waul

ATTACHED

Company C, 1st Tennessee Cavalry, Capt. Richard S. Vandyke

Botetourt Virginia Artillery, Capt. John W. Johnston, Lt. Francis G. Obenchain

Signal Corps Detachment, Lt. C.H. Barrott

FORNEY'S DIVISION
MAJ. GEN. JOHN H. FORNEY

1ST BRIGADE
BRIG. GEN. LOUIS HEBERT

3d Louisiana, Lt. Col. Samuel D. Russell, Maj. David Pierson (w)

21st Louisiana, Col. Isaac W. Patton,

22d Louisiana (detachment), Col. Charles H. Herrick (mw), Lt. Col.   John T. Plattsmier

36th Mississippi, Col. William W. Witherspoon

37th Mississippi, Col. Orlando S. Holland

38th Mississippi, Col. Preston Brent, Capt. Daniel B. Seal

43d Mississippi, Col. Richard Harrison

7th Mississippi Infantry Battalion, Capt. A.M. Dozier

Company C, 2d Alabama Artillery Battalion, Capt. T.K. Emanuel (k),

Lt. John R. Sclater

Appeal Arkansas Artillery, Capt. William N. Hogg, Lt. Christopher C. Scott, Lt. R.N. Cotten

2D BRIGADE

BRIG. GEN. JOHN C. MOORE

37th Alabama, Col. James F. Dowdell

40th Alabama, Col. John H. Higley

42d Alabama, Col. John W. Portis, Lt. Col. Thomas C. Lanier

35th Mississippi, Col. William S. Barry, Lt. Col. Charles R. Jordan

40th Mississippi, Col. Wallace B. Colbert

2d Texas, Col. Ashbel Smith

Companies A,C,D,E, G, I, and K, 1st Mississippi Light Artillery

Col. William T. Withers

Sengstak's Alabama Battery, Capt. Henry H. Sengstak

Company B, Pointe Coupee Artillery, Capt. William A. Davidson

SMITH'S DIVISION
MAJ. GEN. MARTIN LUTHER SMITH

BALDWIN'S BRIGADE

BRIG. GEN. WILLIAM E. BALDWIN

17th Louisiana, Col. Robert Richardson

31st Louisiana, Lt. Col. Sidney H. Griffin (k), Lt. Col. James W. Draughon

4th Mississippi, Lt. Col. Thomas N. Adaire (w), Capt. Thomas P. Nelson

46th Mississippi, Col. Claudius W. Sears

Tobin's Tennessee Battery, Capt. Thomas F. Tobin

SHOUP'S BRIGADE

BRIG. GEN. FRANCIS A. SHOUP

26th Louisiana, Col. Winchester Hall (w), Lt. Col. William C. Crow

27th Louisiana, Col. Leon D. Marks (k), Lt. Col. L.L. McLaurin (k), Capt. Joseph T. Hatch

29th Louisiana, Col. Allen Thomas

McNally's Arkansas Battery, Capt. Francis McNally

VAUGHN'S BRIGADE
BRIG. GEN. JOHN C. VAUGHN
60th Tennessee, Capt. J.W. Bachman
61st Tennessee, Lt. Col. James G. Rose
62d Tennessee, Col. John A. Rowan

***MISSISSIPPI STATE TROOPS*
BRIG. GEN. JEPTHA V. HARRIS
5th Regiment, MST, Col. H.C. Robinson
3d Battalion, MST, Lt. Col. Thomas A. Burgis
**Under General Vaughn's command.

ATTACHED
14th Mississippi Light Artillery Battalion, Maj. Matthew S. Ward
Smyth's Company Mississippi Partisan Rangers, Capt. J.S. Smyth
Signal Corps Detachment, Capt. M.T. Davison

BOWEN'S DIVISION
MAJ. GEN. JOHN S. BOWEN

1ST (MISSOURI) BRIGADE
COL. FRANCIS M. COCKRELL
1st Missouri, Col. Amos C. Riley
2d Missouri, Lt. Col. Pembroke Senteny (k), Maj. Thomas M. Carter
3d Missouri, Lt. Col. Finley L. Hubbard (mw), Col. William L. Gause,
Maj. James K. McDowell
5th Missouri, Lt. Col. Robert S. Bevier, Col. James McCown
6th Missouri, Col. Eugene Erwin (k), Maj. Stephen Cooper
Guibor's Missouri Battery, Capt. Henry Guibor, Lt. William Corkery,
Lt. Cornelius Heffernan
Landis' Missouri Battery, Capt. John C. Landis, Lt. John M. Langan
Wade's Missouri Battery, Lt. Richard C. Walsh

2D BRIGADE
BRIG. GEN. MARTIN E. GREEN (K)
COL. THOMAS P. DOCKERY
15th Arkansas, Lt. Col. William W. Reynolds, Capt. Caleb Davis
19th Arkansas, Col. Thomas P. Dockery, Capt. James K. Norwood
20th Arkansas, Col. D.W. Jones
21st Arkansas, Col. Jordan E. Cravens, Capt. A. Tyler

1st Arkansas Cavalry Battalion (dismounted), Capt. John J. Clark
12th Arkansas Sharpshooters Battalion, Capt. Griff Bayne, Lt. John S. Bell
1st Missouri Cavalry (dismounted), Col. Elijah Gates, Maj. William C. Parker
3d Missouri Cavalry (dismounted), Lt. Col. D. Todd Samuel, Capt. Felix Lotspeich
3d Missouri Battery, Capt. William E. Dawson
Lowe's Missouri Battery, Capt. Schyler Lowe, Lt. Thomas B. Catron

RIVER DEFENSES
COL. EDWARD HIGGINS
1st Louisiana Heavy Artillery, Col. Charles A. Fuller, Lt. Col. Daniel Beltzhoover
8th Louisiana Hevy Artillery Battalion, Maj. Frederick N. Ogden
22d Louisiana (detachment), Capt. Samuel Jones
1st Tennessee Heavy Artillery, Col. Andrew Jackson, Jr.
***Caruthers' Tennessee Battery, Capt. J.B. Caruthers
***Johnston's Tennessee Battery, Capt. T.N. Johnston
***Lynch's Tennessee Battery, Capt. John P. Lynch
Company L, 1st Mississippi Light Artillery, Capt. Samuel C. Bains
***These three companies were attached to the 1st Tennessee Heavy Artillery.

MISCELLANEOUS
54th Alabama, Lt. Joel P. Abney
6th Mississippi (detachment), Maj. J.R. Stevens
City Guards, Capt. E.B. Martin
Signal Corps Detachment, Capt. C.A. King

ARMY OF RELIEF
GEN. JOSEPH E. JOHNSTON

BRECKINRIDGE'S DIVISION
MAJ. GEN. JOHN C. BRECKINRIDGE

ADAM'S BRIGADE
BRIG. GEN. DANIEL W. ADAMS
32d Alabama, Lt. Col. Henry Maury
13th and 20th Louisiana (Consolidated), Col. Augustus Reichard
16th and 25th Louisiana (Consolidated), Col. Daniel Gober
19th Louisiana, Col. Wesley P. Winans
14th Louisiana Sharpshooters Battalion, Maj. John E. Austin

HELM'S BRIGADE
Brig. Gen. Benjamin H. Helm
41st Alabama, Col. Martin L. Stansel
2d Kentucky, Lt. Col. James W. Hewitt
4th Kentucky, Col. Joseph P. Nuckols, Lt. Col. John A. Adair
6th Kentucky, Lt. Col. Martin H. Cofer
9th Kentucky, Col. John W. Caldwell

STOVALL'S BRIGADE
Brig. Gen. Marcellus A. Stovall
1st and 3d Florida (Consolidated), Col. William S. Dilworth
4th Florida, Col. Edward Badger
47th Georgia, Col. George W.M. Williams
60th North Carolina, Col. Washington M. Hardy, Lt. Col. James M. Ray

ARTILLERY
Maj. Rice E. Graves
Johnston (Tennessee) Artillery, Capt. John W. Mebane
Cobb's Kentucky Battery, Capt. Robert Cobb
5th Company, Washington Artillery, Capt. Cuthbert H. Slocomb

FRENCH'S DIVISION
Maj. Gen. Samuel G. French

McNAIR'S BRIGADE
Brig. Gen. Evander McNair

1st Arkansas Mounted Rifles (dismounted), Col. Robert W. Harper,
Lt. Col. Daniel H. Reynolds
2d Arkansas Mounted Rifles (dismounted), Col. J. A. Williamson
4th Arkansas, Col. Henry G. Bunn
25th and 31st Arkansas (Consolidated), Col. Thomas H. McCray
39th North Carolina, Col. David Coleman

MAXEY'S BRIGADE
Brig. Gen. Samuel B. Maxey
4th Louisiana, Lt. Col. William F. Pennington, Col. Samuel E. Hunter
30th Louisiana (battalion), Lt. Col. Thomas Shields
42d Tennessee, Lt. Col. Isaac N. Hulme
46th and 55th Tennessee (Consolidated), Col. Alexander J. Brown,
Lt. Col. Gideon B. Black

48th Tennessee, Col. William M. Voorhees

49th Tennessee, Maj. David A. Lynn

53d Tennessee, Lt. Col. John R. White

1st Texas Sharpshooter Battalion, Maj. James Burnet

EVANS' BRIGADE
BRIG. GEN. NATHAN G. EVANS

17th South Carolina, Col. Fitz William McMasters

18th South Carolina, Col. William H. Wallace

22d South Carolina, Lt. Col. James O'Connell

23d South Carolina, Col. Henry L. Benbow

26th South Carolina, Col. Alexander D. Smith

Holcombe Legion, Lt. Col. William J.Crawley, Maj. Martin G. Zeigler

ARTILLERY
Fenner's (Louisiana) Battery, Capt. Charles E. Fenner

Macbeth (South Carolina) Artillery, Lt. B.A. Jeter

Culpeper's (Sdouth Carolina) Battery, Capt. James F. Culpeper

LORING'S DIVISION
MAJ. GEN. WILLIAM W. LORING

ADAMS' BRIGADE
BRIG. GEN. LLOYD TILGHMAN (K)

COL. ARTHUR E. REYNOLDS

BRIG. GEN. JOHN ADAMS

1st Confederate Battalion, Lt. Col. George H. Forney

6th Mississippi, Col. Robert Lowry

14th Mississippi, Lt. Col. Washington L. Doss

15th Mississippi, Col. Michael Farrell

20th Mississippi, Col. Daniel R. Russell, Lt. Col. William N. Brown

23d Mississippi, Col. Joseph M. Wells

26th Mississippi, Col. Arthur E. Reynolds, Maj. Tully F. Parker

Lookout (Tennessee) Artillery, Capt. Robert L. Barry

BUFORD'S BRIGADE
BRIG. GEN. ABRAHAM BUFORD

27th Alabama, Col. James Jackson

35th Alabama, Col. Edward Goodwin

54th Alabama, Col. Alpheus Baker, Maj. T.H. Shackelford

55th Alabama, Col. John Snodgrass
9th Arkansas, Col. Isaac L. Dunlop
3d Kentucky, Col. Albert P. Thompson
7th Kentucky, Col. Edward Crossland
8th Kentucky, Col. Hylan B. Lyon, Lt. Col. A.R. Shacklett
12th Louisiana, Col. Thomas M. Scott
3d Missouri Cavalry (dismounted), Lt. Col. D. Todd Samuels
Company A, Pointe Coupee Artillery, Capt. Alcide Bouanchaud

FEATHERSTON'S BRIGADE
BRIG. GEN. WINFIELD S. FEATHERSTON
COL. JOHN A. ORR

3d Mississippi, Col. Thomas A. Mellon, Maj. Samuel A. Dyer
22d Mississippi, Col. Frank S. Schaller, Lt. Col. H.J. Reid
31st Mississippi, Col. John A. Orr, Lt. Col. Marcus D.L. Stephens
33d Mississippi, Col. David W. Hurst
1st Mississippi Sharpshooter Battalion, Maj. William A. Rayburn,
Maj. James M. Stigler
Charpentier's Alabama Battery, Capt. Stephen Charpentier
Company C, 14th Mississippi Artillery Battalion, Capt. J. Culbertson

WALKER'S DIVISION
MAJ. GEN. WILLIAM H.T. WALKER

ECTOR'S BRIGADE
BRIG. GEN. MATTHEW D. ECTOR

9th Texas, Lt. Col. Miles A. Dillard
10th Texas Cavalry (dismounted), Lt. Col. C.R. Earp
14th Texas Cavalry (dismounted), Col. John L. Camp
32d Texas Cavalry (dismounted), Col. Julius A. Andrews
Battalion, 43d Mississippi, Capt. M. Pounds
Battalion, 40th Alabama, Maj. Thomas O. Stone
McNally's Arkansas Battery, Lt. F.A. Moore

GREGG'S BRIGADE
BRIG. GEN. JOHN GREGG

3d Tennessee, Col. Calvin H. Walker
10th Tennessee, Lt. Col. William Grace
30th Tennessee, Col. Randall MacGavock (k), Lt. Col. James .J. Turner
41st Tennessee, Col. Robert Farquharson

50th Tennessee, Lt. Col. Thomas W. Beaumont (w), Col. Cyrus A. Sugg
1st Tennessee Infantry Battalion, Maj. Stephen H. Colms
· 7th Texas, Col. Hiram B. Granbury
Bledsoe's Missouri Battery, Capt. Hiram M. Bledsoe

GIST'S BRIGADE
BRIG. GEN. STATES RIGHTS GIST
46th Georgia, Col. Peyton H. Colquitt
8th Georgia, Capt. Zachariah L. Watters
16th South Carolina, Col. James McCullough
24th South Carolina, Col. C.H. Stevens
Ferguson's South Carolina Battery, Capt. T.B. Ferguson

WILSON'S BRIGADE
COL. CLAUDIUS C. WILSON
25th Georgia, Lt. Col. Andrew J. Williams
29th Georgia, Col. William J. Young
30th Georgia, Col. T.W. Mangham
1st Georgia Sharpshooter Battalion, Maj. Arthur Shaaff
4th Louisiana Infantry Battalion, Lt. Col. John McEnery
Martin's Georgia Battery, Lt. Evan P. Howell

CAVALRY DIVISION
BRIG. GEN. WILLIAM H. JACKSON

1ST BRIGADE
BRIG. GEN. GEORGE B. COSBY
1st Mississippi Cavalry, Col. R.A. Pinson
4th Mississippi Cavalry, Col. James Gordon, Maj. J.L. Harris
28th Mississippi Cavalry, Col. Peter B. Starke
Wirt Adams' Mississippi Cavalry, Col. William Wirt Adams
Ballentine's Mississippi Cavalry, Lt. Col. William L. Maxwell
17th Mississippi Cavalry Battalion (State Troops), Maj. Abner C. Steede
Clark's Missouri Battery, Capt. Houston King

2D BRIGADE
BRIG. GEN. JOHN W. WHITFIELD
3d Texas Cavalry, Col. Giles S. Boggess
6th Texas Cavalry, Col. Lawrence S. Ross, Maj. Jack Wharton
9th Texas Cavalry, Col. Dudley W. Jones

27th Texas Cavalry (also called 1st Texas Legion), Lt. Col. John H. Broocks
Bridge's Arkansas Cavalry Battalion, Maj. H.W. Bridges
ESCORTS AND GUARDS
Company A, 7th Tennessee Cavalry, Capt. W.F. Taylor
Independent Company Louisiana Cavalry, Capt. J.Y. Webb
Provost Guard (Company D 4th Mississippi Cavalry), Capt. James Ruffin

RESERVE ARTILLERY
Maj. W.C. Preston
Columbus Georgia Battery, Capt. Edward Croft
Durrive's Louisana Battery, Capt. E. Durrive, Jr.
Battery B, Palmetto South Carolina Artillery, Capt. J. Wates

TRANS-MISSISSIPPI DEPARTMENT
LT. GEN. E. KIRBY SMITH

DISTRICT OF WESTERN LOUISIANA
MAJ. GEN. RICHARD TAYLOR

WALKER'S DIVISION
Maj. Gen. John G. Walker

McCULLOCH'S BRIGADE
Brig. Gen. Henry E. McCulloch
16th Texas, Col. George Flournoy
17th Texas, Col. R.T.P. Allen
19th Texas, Col. Richard Waterhouse
16th Texas Cavalry (dismounted), Lt. Col. E.P. Gregg (w), Maj. W.W. Diamond (w),
Capt. J.D. Woods
Edgar's Battery, Capt. William Edgar

HAWES' BRIGADE
Brig. Gen. James M. Hawes
13th Texas Cavalry (dismounted), Lt. Col. A.F. Crawford
12th Texas, Col. O. Young
18th Texas, Lt. Col. D.B. Culbertson
22d Texas, Col. R. Hubbard
Halderman's Battery, Capt. Horace Halderman

RANDAL'S BRIGADE
COL. HORACE RANDAL
11th Texas, Col. O.M. Roberts
14th Texas, Col. E. Clark
28th Texas Cavalry (dismounted), Col. E.H. Baxter
6th Texas Cavalry Battalion (dismounted), Maj. R.S. Gould
Daniels' Battery, Capt. J.M. Daniels

TAPPAN'S BRIGADE
BRIG. GEN. JAMES C. TAPPAN
27th Arkansas, Col. J.R. Shaler
33d Arkansas, Col. H.L. Grinsted
38th Arkansas, Col. R.G. Shaver

CAVALRY (NOT BRIGADED)
13th Louisiana Cavalry Battalion, Col. Frank A. Bartlett
15th Louisiana Cavalry Battalion, Lt. Col. Isaac F. Harrison

PARSON'S CAVALRY BRIGADE
COL. WILLIAM H. PARSONS
12th Texas Cavalry, Lt. Col. A.B. Burleson
21st Texas Cavalry, Col. B.W. Carter
Pratt's Texas Battery, Capt. J.H. Pratt

APPENDIX B

ORGANIZATION OF UNION FORCES

ARMY OF THE TENNESSEE
MAJ. GEN. ULYSSES S. GRANT

ESCORT
Company A, 4th Illinois Cavalry, Capt. Embury D. Osband

ENGINEERS
1st Battalion, Engineer Regiment of the West, Maj. William Tweeddale

THIRTEENTH CORPS
MAJ. GEN. JOHN A. MCCLERNAND (RELIEVED)
MAJ. GEN. EDWARD O. C. ORD

ESCORT
Company L, 3d Illinois Cavalry, Capt. David R. Sparks

PIONEERS
Independent Company, Kentucky Infantry, Capt. William F. Patterson

NINTH DIVISION
BRIG. GEN. PETER OSTERHAUS (W)
BRIG. GEN. ALBERT L. LEE
BRIG. GEN. PETER OSTERHAUS

1ST BRIGADE
BRIG. GEN. THEOPHILUS T. GARRARD
BRIG. GEN. ALBERT L. LEE
COL. JAMES KEIGWIN
118th Illinois, Col. John G. Fonda
49th Indiana, Col. James Keigwin, Maj. Arthur J. Hawhe, Lt. Col . Joseph H. Thornton
69th Indiana, Col. Thomas W. Bennett, Lt. Col. Oran Perry
7th Kentucky, Maj. H.W. Adams, Lt. Col. John Lucas, Col. Reuben May
120th Ohio, Col. Marcus M. Spiegel

2D BRIGADE
COL. LIONEL A. SHELDON
COL. DANIEL LINDSEY
54th Indiana, Col. Fielding Mansfield
22d Kentucky, Lt. Col. George W. Monroe
16th Ohio, Capt. Eli W. Botsford, Maj. Milton Mills
42d Ohio, Lt. Col. Don A. Pardee, Maj. William H. Williams, Col.   Lionel Sheldon
114th Ohio, Col. John Cradlebaugh, (w), Lt. Col. John H. Kelly

CAVALRY
2d Illinois (5 Companies), Lt. Col. Daniel B. Bush, Jr.
3d Illinois Cavalry (3 Companies), Col. John L. Campbell
6th Missouri Cavalry (7 Companies), Col. Clark Wright

ARTILLERY
CAPT. JACOB T. FOSTER
7th Michigan Light Artillery, Capt. Charles H. Lanphere
1st Battery, Wisconsin Light Artillery, Lt. Charles B. Kimball, Lt Oscar F. Nutting

TENTH DIVISION
BRIG. GEN. ANDREW J. SMITH

ESCORT
Company C, 4th Indiana Cavalry, Capt. Andrew P. Gallagher

1ST BRIGADE
BRIG. GEN. STEPHEN G. BURBRIDGE
16th Indiana, Col. Thomas J. Lucas, Maj. James H. Redfield
60th Indiana, Col. Richard Owen
67th Indiana, Lt. Col. Theodore E. Buehler
83d Ohio, Col. Frederick W. Moore
96th Ohio, Col. Jsoeph W. Vance
23d Wisconsin, Col. Joshua J. Guppey, Lt. Col. William F. Vilas

2D BRIGADE

COL. WILLIAM J. LANDRUM

77th Illinois, Col. David P. Grier

97th Illinois, Col. Friend S. Rutherford, Lt. Col. Lewis D. Martin

130th Illinois, Col. Nathaniel Niles

19th Kentucky, Lt. Col. John Cowan, Maj. M. V. Evans (k), Capt. Josiah J. Mann

48th Ohio, Lt. Col. Job R. Parker (w), Col. Peter Sullivan, Capt. J.W. Lindsey

ARTILLERY

Chicago Merchantile Battery, Illinois Light Artillery, Capt. Patrick H. White

17th Battery, Ohio Light Artillery, Capt. Ambrose A. Blount,

Capt. Charles S. Rice

TWELFTH DIVISION

BRIG. GEN. ALVIN P. HOVEY

ESCORT

Company C, 1st Indiana Cavalry, Lt. James L. Carey

1ST BRIGADE

BRIG. GEN. GEORGE F. MCGINNIS

COL. WILLIAM T. SPICELY

11th Indiana, Col. Daniel Macauley (w), Lt. Col. William W. Darnell

24th Indiana, Col. William T. Spicely (w), Lt. Col. R.F. Barter

34th Indiana, Col. Robert A. Cameron, Lt. Col. William Swaim (mw),

Maj. Robert A. Jones, Col. Robert A. Cameron

46th Indiana, Col. Thomas H. Bringhurst

29th Wisconsin, Col. Charles R. Gill, Lt. Col. William A. Greene

2D BRIGADE

COL. JAMES R. SLACK

87th Illinois, Col. John E. Whiting

47th Indiana, Lt. Col. John A. McLaughlin

24th Iowa, Col. Eber C. Byam, Lt. Col. John Q. Wilds

28th Iowa, Col. John Connell

56th Oho, Col. William H. Raynor

ARTILLERY
Company A, 1st Missouri Light Artillery, Capt. George W. Schofield
2d Battery, Ohio Light Artillery, Lt. Augustus Beach
16th Battery Ohio Light Artillery, Capt. James A. Mitchell (mw), Lt. George Murdock,
Lt. Russell P. Twist

FOURTEENTH DIVISION
BRIG. GEN. EUGENE A. CARR

ESCORT
Company G, 3d Illinois Cavalry, Capt. Enos McPhial (k), Capt. Samuel S. Marrett

1ST BRIGADE
BRIG. GEN. WILLIAM P. BENTON
COL. HENRY D. WASHBURN
COL. DAVID SHUNK
33d Illinois, Col. Charles E. Lippincott (w),
99th Illinois, Col. George W.K. Bailey
8th Indiana, Col. David Shunk, Maj. Thomas J. Brady
18th Indiana, Col. Henry D. Washburn, Capt. Jonathan H. Williams
1st U.S. Infantry (Siege Guns), Maj. Maurice Maloney

2D BRIGADE
COL. CHARLES L. HARRIS
COL. WILLIAM M. STONE
BRIG. GEN. MICHAEL K. LAWLER
21st Iowa Infantry, Col. Samuel Merrill (w), Lt. Col. Cornelius W. Dunlap (k),
Maj. Salue G. Van Anda
22d Iowa, Col. William M. Stone (w), Lt. Col. Harvey Graham (w and c),
Maj. Joseph B. Atherton, Capt. Charles N. Lee
23d Iowa, Col. William H. Kinsoman (k), Col. Samuel L. Glasgow
11th Wisconsin, Lt. Col. Charles A. Wood, Col. Charles L. Harris, Maj. Arthur Platt

ARTILLERY
Company A, 2d Illinois Light Artillery, Lt. Frank B. Fenton, Capt. Peter Davidson
1st Battery, Indiana Light Artillery, Capt. Martin Klauss

FIFTEENTH CORPS
MAJ. GEN. WILLIAM T. SHERMAN

FIRST DIVISION
MAJ. GEN. FREDERICK STEELE

1ST BRIGADE
COL. FRANCIS H. MANTER
COL. BERNARD G. FARRAR
13th Illinois, Col. Adam B. Gorgas
27th Missouri, Col. Thomas Curly
29th Missouri, Col. James Peckham
30th Missouri, Lt. Col. Otto Schadt
31st Missouri, Col. Thomas C. Fletcher, Maj. Frederick Jaensch,
Lt. Col. Samuel P. Simpson
32d Missouri, Maj. Abraham J. Seay

2D BRIGADE
COL. CHARLES R. WOODS
25th Iowa, Col. George A. Stone
31st Iowa, Col. William Smith
3d Missouri, Lt. Col. Theodore M. Meumann
12th Missouri, Col. Hugo Wangelin
17th Missouri, Col. Francis Hassendeubel (mw), Lt. Col. John F.   Cramer
76th Ohio, Lt. Col. William B. Woods

3D BRIGADE
BRIG. GEN. JOHN M. THAYER
4th Iowa, Col. James A. Williamson, Lt. Col. George Burton
9th Iowa, Maj. Don A. Carpenter, Capt. Frederick S. Washburn (k),
Col. David Carskaddon
26th Iowa, Col. Milo Smith
30th Iowa, Col. Charles H. Abbott (k), Lt. Col. William M.G. Torrence

CAVALRY
Kane County (Illinois) Company, Lt. Thomas J. Beebe
Company D, 3d Illinois Cavalry, Lt. Jonathan Kershner

ARTILLERY

1st Battery, Iowa Light Artillery, Capt. Henry H. Griffiths
Company F, 2d Missouri Light Artillery, Capt. Clemens Landgraeber
4th Battery, Ohio Light Artillery, Capt. Louis Hoffmann

SECOND DIVISION
MAJ. GEN. FRANK P. BLAIR, JR.

1ST BRIGADE
COL. GILES A. SMITH
113th Illinois, Col. George B. Hoge, Lt. Col. John W. Paddock
116th Illinois, Col. Nathan W. Tupper
6th Missouri, Lt. Col. Ira Boutell, Col. James H. Blood
8th Missouri, Lt. Col. David C. Coleman
13th United States, Capt. Edward Washington (mw), Capt. Charles Ewing,
Capt. Charles C. Smith

2D BRIGADE
COL. THOMAS KILBY SMITH
BRIG. GEN. JOSEPH A.J. LIGHTBURN
55th Illinois, Col. Oscar Malmborg
127th Illinois, Col. Hamilton N. Eldridge
83d Indiana, Col. Benjamin J. Spooner
54th Ohio, Lt. Col. Cyrus W. Fisher
57th Ohio, Col. Americus V. Rice (w), Lt. Col. Samuel R. Mott

3D BRIGADE
BRIG. GEN. HUGH EWING
30th Ohio, Lt. Col. George H. Hildt, Col. Theodore Jones
37th Ohio, Lt. Col. Louis von Blessingh (w), Maj. Charles Hipp, Col. Edward Siber
47th Ohio, Col. Augustus C. Parry
4th West Virginia, Col. James H. Dayton

CAVALRY
Companies A and B, Thielemann's (Illinois) Battalion,
Capt. Milo Thielemann
Company C, 10th Missouri Cavalry, Capt. Daniel W. Ballou, Lt. Benjamin Joel

ARTILLERY

Company A, 1st Illinois Light Artillery, Capt. Peter P. Wood

Company B, 1st Illinois Light Artillery, Capt. Samuel E. Barrett,
Lt. Israel P. Rumsey

Company H, 1st Illinois Light Artillery, Capt. Levi W. Hart

8th Battery, Ohio Light Artillery, Capt. James F. Putnam

THIRD DIVISION
BRIG. GEN. JAMES M. TUTTLE

1ST BRIGADE

BRIG. GEN. RALPH P. BUCKLAND

COL. WILLIAM L. MCMILLEN

114th Illinois, Col. James W. Judy

93d Indiana, Col. De Witt C. Thomas

72d Ohio, Lt. Col. Le Roy Crockett (w), Maj. Charles G. Eaton

95th Ohio, Col. William L. McMillen, Lt. Col. Jefferson Brumback

2D BRIGADE

BRIG. GEN. JOSEPH A. MOWER

47th Illinois, Col. John N. Cromwell (k), Lt. Col. Samuel R. Baker

5th Minnesota, Col. Lucius F. Hubbard

11th Missouri, Col. Andrew J. Weber (mw), Lt. Col. William L. Barnum

8th Wisconsin, Col. George W. Robbins

3D BRIGADE

BRIG. GEN. CHARLES L. MATTHIES

COL. JOSEPH J. WOODS

8th Iowa, Col. James L. Geddes

12th Iowa, Col. Joseph J. Woods, Lt. Col. Samuel R. Edington

35th Iowa, Col. Sylvester G. Hill

CAVALRY

4TH IOWA, LT. COL. SIMEON D. SWAN

ARTILLERY

CAPT. NELSON T. SPOOR

Company E, 1st Illinois Light Artillery, Capt. Allen C. Waterhouse

2d Battery, Iowa Light Artillery, Lt. Joseph R. Reed

SEVENTEENTH CORPS
MAJ. GEN. JAMES B. McPHERSON

ESCORT
4th Company Ohio Cavalry, Capt. John S. Foster

THIRD DIVISION
MAJ. GEN. JOHN A. LOGAN

ESCORT
Company A, 2d Illinois Cavalry, Lt. William B. Cummins

1ST BRIGADE
BRIG. GEN. JOHN E. SMITH
BRIG. GEN. MORTIMER D. LEGGETT
20th Illinois, Lt. Col. Evan Richards (k), Maj. Daniel Bradley
31st Illinois, Col. Edwin S. McCook (w), Lt. Col. John D. Rees (mw),
Maj. Robert N. Pearson
45th Illinois, Col. Jasper A. Maltby
124th Illinois, Col. Thomas J. Sloan
23d Indiana, Lt. Col. William P. Davis

2D BRIGADE
BRIG. GEN. ELIAS S. DENNIS
BRIG. GEN. MORTIMER D. LEGGETT
COL. MANNING F. FORCE
30th Illinois, Lt. Col. Warren Shedd
20th Ohio, Col. Manning F. Force, Capt. Francis M. Shaklee
68th Ohio, Lt. Col. John S. Snook (k), Col. Robert K. Scott
78th Ohio, Lt. Col. Greenberry F. Wiles

3D BRIGADE
BRIG. GEN. JOHN D. STEVENSON
8th Illinois, Col. John P. Post, Lt. Col. Robert H. Sturgess
17th Illinois, Lt. Col. Francis M. Smith, Maj. Frank F. Peats
81st Illinois, Col. James J. Dollins (k), Lt. Col. Franklin Campbell
7th Missouri, Maj. Edwin Wakefield, Lt. Col. William S. Oliver (w),
Capt. Robert Buchanan, Capt. William B. Collins
32d Ohio, Col. Benjamin F. Potts

ARTILLERY

MAJ. CHARLES J. STOLBRAND

Company D, 1st Illinois Light Artillery, Capt. Henry A. Rogers (k),
Lt. George J. Wood, Capt. Frederick Sparrestrom
Company G, 2d Illinois Light Artillery, Capt. Frederick Sparrestrom, Lt. John W. Lowell
Company L, 2d Illinois Light Artillery, Capt. William H. Bolton
8th Battery, Michigan Light Artillery, Capt. Samuel De Golyer (mw),
Lt. Theodore W. Lockwood
3d Battery, Ohio Light Artillery, Capt. William S. Williams
Yost's Independent Ohio Battery, Capt. T. Yost

SIXTH DIVISION
BRIG. GEN. JOHN MCARTHUR

ESCORT
Company G, 1st Illinois Cavalry, Lt. Stephen S. Tripp

2D BRIGADE

BRIG. GEN. THOMAS E.G. RANSOM

11th Illinois, Lt. Col. Garrett Nevins (k), Lt. Col. James H. Coates
72d Illinois, Col. Frederick A. Starring
95th Illinois, Col. Thomas W. Humphrey (w), Lt. Col. Leander Blanden
14th Wisconsin, Col. Lyman M. Ward
17th Wisconsin, Lt. Col. Thomas McMahon, Col. Adam G. Malloy

3D BRIGADE

COL. WILLIAM HALL

COL. ALEXANDER CHAMBERS

11th Iowa, Lt. Col. John C. Abercrombie, Col. William Hall
13th Iowa, Col. John Shane
15th Iowa, Col. William W. Belknap
16th Iowa, Maj. W. Purcell, Lt. Col. Addison H. Sanders

ARTILLERY

MAJ. THOMAS D. MAURICE

Company F, 2d Illinois Light Artillery, Capt. John W. Powell
1st Battery, Minnesota Light Artillery, Lt. Henry Hunter, Capt. William Z. Clayton
Company C, 1st Missouri Light Artillery, Capt. Charles Mann
10th Battery, Ohio Light Artillery, Capt. Hamilton B. White, Lt. William L. Newcomb

SEVENTH DIVISION
BRIG. GEN. MARCELLUS M. CROCKER
BRIG. GEN. ISAAC F. QUINBY
BRIG. GEN. JOHN E. SMITH

ESCORT
Company F, 4th Missouri Cvalry, Lt. Alexander Mueller

1ST BRIGADE
COL. JOHN B. SANBORN
48th Indiana, Col. Norman Eddy
59th Indiana, Col. Jesse I. Alexander
4th Minnesota Infantry, Lt. Col. John E. Tourtellotte
18th Wisconsin, Col. Gabriel Bouck

2D BRIGADE
COL. SAMUEL HOLMES
COL. GREEN B. RAUM
56th Illinois, Col. Green B. Raum, Capt. Pickney J. Welsh
17th Iowa, Col. David B. Hillis, Col. Clark R. Weaver, Maj. John F.Walden
10th Missouri, Lt. Col. Leonidas Horney (k), Maj. Francis C. Deimling
Company E, 24th Missouri, Lt. Daniel Driscoll
80th Ohio, Col. Matthias H. Bartilson, Maj. Prentis Metham

3D BRIGADE
COL. GEORGE B. BOOMER (K)
COL. HOLDEN PUTNAM
93d Illinois, Col. Holden Putnam, Lt. Col. Nicholas C. Buswell
5th Iowa, Lt. Col. Ezekial S. Sampson, Col. Jabez Banbury
10th Iowa, Col. William E. Small
26th Missouri, Capt. Benjamin D. Dean

ARTILLERY
CAPT. FRANK C. SANDS
CAPT. HENRY DILLION
Company M, 1st Missouri Light Artillery, Lt. Junius W. MacMurray
11th Battery, Ohio Light Artillery, Lt. Fletcher E. Armstrong
6th Battery, Wisconsin Light Artillery, Capt. Henry Dillon, Lt. Samuel F. Clark
12th Battery, Wisconsin Light Artillery, Capt. William Zickerick

NINTH CORPS (Detachment)
MAJ. GEN. JOHN G. PARKE

FIRST DIVISION
Brig. Gen. Thomas Welsh

1ST BRIGADE
Col. Henry Bowman

36th Massachusetts, Lt. Col. John B. Norton
17th Michigan, Lt. Col. Constant Luce
27th Michigan, Col. Dorus M. Fox
45th Pennsylvania, Col. John I. Curtin

3D BRIGADE
Col. Daniel Leasure

2d Michigan, Col. William Humphrey
8th Michigan, Col. Frank Graves
20th Michigan, Lt. Col. W. Huntington Smith
79th New York, Col. David Morrison
100th Pennsylvania, Lt. Col. Mathew M. Dawson

ARTILLERY
Company D, 1st Pennsylvania Light Artillery, Capt. G.W. Durell

SECOND DIVISION
Brig. Gen. Robert B. Potter

1ST BRIGADE
Col. Simon G. Griffin

6th New Hampshire, Lt. Col. Henry H. Pearson
9th New Hampshire, Col. Herbert B. Titus
7th Rhode Island, Col. Zenas R. Bliss

2D BRIGADE
Brig. Gen. Edward Ferrero

35th Massachusetts, Col. Sumner Carruth
11th New Hampshire, Lt. Col. Moses N. Collins
51st New York, Col. Charles W. LeGendre
51st Pennsylvania, Col. John F. Hartranft

3D BRIGADE
COL. BENJAMIN C. CHRIST
39th Massachusetts, Lt. Col. Joseph H. Barnes
46th New York, Col. Joseph Gerhardt
50th Pennsylvania, Lt. Col. Thomas S. Brenholtz

ARTILLERY
Company L, 2d New York Light Artillery, Capt. Jacob Roemer

CORPS ARTILLERY
COMPANY E, 2D U.S. ARTILLERY, LT. SAMUEL N. BENJAMIN

SIXTEENTH CORPS
MAJ. GEN. CADWALLADER C. WASHBURN

FIRST DIVISION
BRIG. GEN. WILLIAM SOOY SMITH

ESCORT
Company B, 7th Illinois Cavalry, Capt. Henry C. Forbes

1ST BRIGADE
COL. JOHN M. LOOMIS
26th Illinois, Maj. John B. Harris
90th Illinois, Col. Timothy O'Meara
12th Indiana, Col. Reuben Williams
100th Indiana, Lt. Col. Albert Heath

2D BRIGADE
COL. STEPHEN G. HICKS
40th Illinois Maj. Hiram W. Hall
103d Illinois, Col. Willard A. Dickerman
15th Michigan, Col. John M. Oliver
46th Ohio, Col. Charles C. Walcutt

3D BRIGADE
Col. Joseph R. Cockerill
97th Indiana, Col. Robert F. Catterson
99th Indiana, Col. Alexander Fowler
53d Ohio, Col. Wells S. Jones
70th Ohio, Maj. William B. Brown

4TH BRIGADE
Col. William W. Sanford
48th Illinois, Lt. Col. Lucien Greathouse
6th Iowa, Col. John M. Corse

ARTILLERY
Capt. William Cogswell
Company F, 1st Illinois Light Artillery, Capt. John T. Cheney
Company I, 1st Illinois Light Artillery, Lt. William N. Lansing
Cogswell's Battery, Illinois Light Artillery, Lt. Henry G. Eddy
6th Battery, Indiana Light Artillery, Capt. Michael Muller

FOURTH DIVISION
Brig. Gen. Jacob Lauman

1ST BRIGADE
Col. Isaac Pugh
41st Illinois, Lt. Col. John H. Nale
53d Illinois, Lt. Col. Seth C. Earl
3d Iowa, Col. Aaron Brown
33d Wisconsin, Col. Jonathan B. Moore

2D BRIGADE
Col. Cyrus Hall
14th Illinois, Lt. Col. William Cairn, Capt. Augustus H. Corman
15th Illinois, Col. George C. Rogers
46th Illinois, Col. Benjamin Dornblaser
76th Illinois, Col. Samuel T. Busey
53d Indiana, Col. Walter Q. Gresham

3D BRIGADE
COL. GEORGE E. BRYANT
COL. AMORY K. JOHNSON
28th Illinois, Maj. Hinman Rhodes
32d Illinois, Col. John Logan, Lt. Col. William Hunter
12th Wisconsin, Lt. Col. DeWitt C. Poole, Col. George E. Bryant

CAVALRY
Companies F and I, 15th Illinois, Maj. James G. Wilson

ARTILLERY
CAPT. GEORGE C. GUMBART
Company E, 2d Illinois Light Artillery, Lt. George L. Nispel
Company K, 2d Illinois Light Artillery, Capt. Benjamin F. Rodgers
5th Battery, Ohio Light Artillery, Lt. Anthony Burton
7th Battery, Ohio Light Artillery, Capt. Silas A. Burnap
15th Battery Ohio Light Artillery, Capt. Edward Spear, Jr.

PROVISIONAL DIVISION
BRIG. GEN. NATHAN KIMBALL

ENGELMANN'S BRIGADE
COL. ADOLPH ENGELMANN
43d Illinois, Lt. Col. Adolph Dengler
61st Illinois, Maj. Simon P. Ohr
106th Illinois, Maj. John M. Hunt
12th Michigan, Col. William H. Graves

RICHMOND'S BRIGADE
COL. JONATHAN RICHMOND
18th Illinois, Col. Daniel H. Brush
54th Illinois, Col. Greenville M. Mitchell
126th Illinois, Maj. William W. Wilshire
22d Ohio, Col. Oliver Wood

MONTGOMERY'S BRIGADE
COL. MILTON MONTGOMERY
40th Iowa, Col. John A. Garrett
3d Minnesota, Col. Chauncey W. Griggs
25th Wisconsin, Lt. Col. Samuel J. Nasmith
27th Wisconsin, Col. Conrad Krez

HERRON'S DIVISION
MAJ. GEN. FRANCIS J. HERRON

1ST BRIGADE
BRIG. GEN. WILLIAM VANDEVER
37th Illinois, Col. John C. Black
26th Indiana, Col. John G. Clark
20th Iowa, Col. William McE. Dye
34th Iowa, Col. George W. Clark
38th Iowa, Col. Henry Hughes
Company E, 1st Missouri Light Artillery, Capt. Nelson Cole
Company F, 1st Missouri Light Artillery, Capt. Joseph Foust

2D BRIGADE
BRIG. GEN. WILLIAM W. ORME
94th Illinois, Col. John McNulta
19th Iowa, Lt. Col. Daniel Kent
20th Wisconsin, Col. Henry Bertram
Company B, 1st Missouri Light Artillery, Capt. Martin Welfley

UNATTACHED CAVALRY
COL. CYRUS BUSSEY
5th Illinois Cavalry, Maj. Thomas A. Apperson
3d Iowa Cavalry (six companies), Maj. Oliver H.P. Scott
4th Iowa Cavalry, Lt. Col. Simneon D. Swan
2d Wisconsin Cavalry (seven companies), Col. Thomas Stephens

DISTRICT OF NORTHEAST LOUISIANA
BRIG. GEN. JEREMIAH C. SULLIVAN
BRIG. GEN. ELIAS S. DENNIS

DETACHED BRIGADE
COL. GEORGE W. NEELEY
63d Illionis, Col. Joseph B. McCown
108th Illinois, Lt. Col. Charles Turner
120th Illinois, Col. George W. McKeaig
131st Illinois, Col. George W. Neeley, Maj. Joseph L. Purvis
10th Illinois Cavalry (4 companies), Maj. Elvis P. Shaw

AFRICAN BRIGADE

(Post of Milliken's Bend)

Col. Isaac F. Shephard

Col. Hermann Leib

Lt. Col. Charles J. Paine

8th Louisiana (African Descent), Col. Hiram Scofield

9th Louisiana (African Descent), Col. Hermann Lieb, Maj. Erastus N. Owens,
Lt. Col. Charles J. Paine

11th Louisiana (African Descent), Col. Edwin W. Chamberlain, Lt. Col. Cyrus Sears

13th Louisiana (African Descent), Lt. H. Knoll

1st Mississippi (African Descent), Lt. Col. A. Watson Webber

3d Mississippi (African Descent), Col. Richard H. Ballinger

(Post of Goodrich's Landing)

Col. William F. Wood

1st Arkansas (African Descent), Lt. Col. James W. Campbell

10th Louisiana (African Descent), Lt. Col. Frederick M. Crandall

POST OF LAKE PROVIDENCE

(1st Brigade, 6th Division, XVII Corps)

Brig. Gen. Hugh T. Reid

1st Kansas, Col. William Y. Roberts

16th Wisconsin, Col. Benjamin Allen

SELECTED BIBLIOGRAPHY

Anderson, Ephriam McD. *Memoirs: Historical and Personal; Including the Campaigns of the First Missouri Confederate Brigade.* Edited by Edwin C. Bearss. Dayton, OH: 1972.

Ballard, Michael. *Pemberton: A Biography.* Jackson, MS: 1991.

Bearss, Edwin C. *The Vicksburg Campaign.* 3 vols. Dayton, OH: 1985–1986.

_____. *The Battle of Jackson/The Siege of Jackson.* Baltimore: 1981.

Bevier, Robert S. *History of the First and Second Missouri Confederate Brigades, 1861–1865.* St. Louis: 1879.

Blessington, Joseph P. *The Campaigns of Walker's Texas Division.* Austin, TX: 1968.

Brown, D. Alexander. *Grierson's Raid.* Urbana, IL: 1954.

Carter, Samuel, III. *The Final Fortress: The Campaign for Vicksburg, 1862–1863.* New York: 1980.

Fiske, John. *The Mississippi Valley in the Civil War.* Cambridge, MA: 1900.

Foster, William L. *Vicksburg: Southern City Under Siege.* New Orleans: 1982.

Grant, Ulysses S. *Personal Memoirs of U. S. Grant.* 2 vols. New York: 1885.

Greene, Francis V. *The Mississippi.* New York: 1882.

Hoehling, A. A. *Vicksburg: 47 Days of Siege.* Englewood Cliffs, NJ: 1969.

Johnson, Robert U. and Clarence C. Buel, eds. *Battles and Leaders f the Civil War.* 4 vols. New York: 1884–1889.

Korn, Jerry. *War on the Mississippi.* Alexandria: 1985.

Leckie, William H. and Shirley A. *Unlikely Warriors: General Benjamin H. Grierson and His Family.* Norman, OK: 1984.

Lewis, Lloyd. *Sherman: Fighting Prophet.* New York: 1932.

Loughborough, Mary. *My Cave Life in Vicksburg.* Spartanburg, SC: 1976.

Oldroyd, Osborn. *A Soldier's Story of the Siege of Vicksburg.* Springfield, IL: 1885.

Pemberton, John C. *Pemberton: Defender of Vicksburg.* Chapel Hill, NC: 1942.

Porter, David Dixon. *Incidents and Anecdotes of the Civil War.* New York, 1885.

Stone, Kate. *Brokenburn: The Journal of Kate Stone.* Edited by John Q. Anderson. Baton Rouge: 1955.

Surby, Richard. *Grierson Raids.* Chicago: 1865.

Taylor, Richard. *Destruction and Reconstruction.* New York: 1879

United States War Department. *War of the Rebellion: Official Records of the Union and Confederate Armies.* 128 vols. Washington, D.C.: 1880–1901.

_____. *War of the Rebellion: Official Records of the Union and Confederate Navies.* 31 vols. Washington, D.C.: 1895–1929.

Walker, Peter F. *Vicksburg: A People at War.* Chapel Hill: 1960

Wells, Seth J. *The Siege of Vicksburg from the Diary of Seth J. Wells, Including Weeks of Preparation and of Occupation After the Surrender.* Detroit, 1915.

Winschel, Terrence J. *Triumph and Defeat: The Vicksburg Campaign.* Mason City, IA: 1999.

ABOUT THE BIOGRAPHICAL SKETCHES

The biographical sketches and vignettes that accompany the photographs in this volume were derived from numerous sources and prepared by David Coffey with contributions from Grady McWhiney, Terrence J. Winschel, Paul Cochran, and Charles Grear.

SELECTED REFERENCE WORKS

Boatner, Mark M, III. *The Civil War Dictionary.* Revised edition. New York: David McKay Company, 1988.

Current, Richard N. ed. *Encyclopedia of the Confederacy.* 4 vols. New York: Simon & Schuster, 1993.

Davis, William C. ed. *The Confederate General.* 6 vols. National Historical Society, 1991.

Sifakis, Stewart. *Who Was Who in the Union.* New York: Facts on File, 1988.

_____. *Who Was Who in the Confederacy.* New York: Facts on File, 1988.

Warner, Ezra. *Generals in Gray: Lives of the Confederate* Commanders. Baton Rouge: Louisiana State University Press, 1959.

_____. *Generals in Blue: Lives of the Union Commanders.* Baton Rouge: Louisiana State University Press, 1964.

PHOTO CREDITS

We gratefully acknowledge the cooperation of the United States Army Military History Institute at Carlisle Barracks, Pennsylvania, for photographs of Francis P. Blair, Jr.,David Glasgow Farragut, Joseph E. Johnston, John A. Logan, James B. McPherson, David D. Porter, Richard Taylor, and Earl Van Dorn.

We credit the Library of Congress for the photographs of Ulysses S.Grant, John Gregg, and William T. Sherman.

We are grateful to the Harold B. Simpson Confederate Research Center in Hillsboro, Texas for the photograph of Henry E. McCulloch.

The photographs of John S. Bowen, Francis Marion Cockrell, John C. Pemberton, and Lloyd Tilghman are from *Generals in Gray: Lives of the Confederate Commanders*, by Ezra J. Warner (Louisiana State University Press, 1959).

The photographs of Benjamin Henry Grierson and John A. McClernand are from *Generals in Blue: Lives of the Union Commanders*, by Ezra J. Warner (Louisiana State University Press, 1964).

The photographs of Abraham, Emma Balfour, Orion P. Howe, Mary Loughborough, Old Abe, and Coonskin's Tower are from the collection at Vicksburg National Military Park.

INDEX